LEVERAGED
Learning

ADVANCE PRAISE FOR
LEVERAGED LEARNING

"*Leveraged Learning* is a well-crafted, compelling examination and re-imagination of education. In the face of our consternation about the future of work and societal turmoil, Danny Iny gives us a path toward a smarter and more capable world."

–RANDY KOMISAR, partner at Kleiner Perkins Caufield & Byers, former CEO of LucasArts Entertainment and Crystal Dynamics, former Stanford professor, and best-selling author of *The Monk and the Riddle* and *Getting to Plan B*

"*Leveraged Learning* is a must-read for anyone looking to spread ideas. In a world of shrinking attention spans, education is experiencing a revolution. Danny Iny has his finger on the pulse of what's to come, and a gift for translating complicated, jargon-heavy theory into simple and engaging concepts. The result is a compelling, practical and important guide to teaching in the age of distraction."

–RON FRIEDMAN, PH.D., best-selling author of *The Best Place to Work*

"A prescient look at where the learning industry is headed, and the implications for both students and professionals."

–JEFF COBB, co-founder of Tagoras, and author of *Leading the Learning Revolution*

"If you are anything like me, your degree alone didn't prepare you for the job you have today. Most likely, you don't even work in the same field as your original degree! Danny Iny isn't the first to make this observation, or to question the path that most educational institutions are on. But no one has laid out a cogent argument for a meaningful alternative for achieving true learning that best serves the student. Until now. If you care about our broken education system, you most read *Leveraged Learning*."

–ABE CRYSTAL, CEO of Ruzuku

"Danny takes an intriguing exploration into the problems with the current models for learning, and gives some thoughtful ideas for where we need to go next."

–RANDY GAGE, *New York Times* best-selling author of *Risky is the New Safe* and *Mad Genius*

"My reputation is in part because of my education. And I make my living by being an educator, teaching leaders and managers around the world. And I'm in a perpetual state of anxiety about the future of education. Because I know it's changing... I'm just not sure exactly how, or how fast. Danny Iny is my trusted guide across a treacherous landscape."

–MICHAEL BUNGAY STANIER, author of the *WSJ*-bestseller, *The Coaching Habit*

"This is the end of expensive and worthless degrees. As an employer and a lifelong learner, I feel Danny has concisely identified the challenges facing post-secondary both in usefulness to the student and as a signal to employers. His solution, while not simple, will lead to employees who are highly capable, well educated for the task at hand and skilled at keeping their knowledge current to support their current and future growth needs."

–DAVE LAKHANI, CEO of Bold Approach, best-selling author of *Persuasion: The Art of Getting What You Want*

"Danny Iny has done the hard work of studying the true future of learning, and outlines the strategies and tactics to make sure you don't get left behind."

–DAVID BURKUS, associate professor at Oral Roberts University, and best-selling author of *Friend of a Friend* and *Under New Management*

"*Leveraged Learning* is a tour de force of education—how it evolved, what it delivered and where it is going. We all know that higher education is 'broken,' but Danny give us a penetrating insight into how it is broken and why it is broken. He identifies the four major transformations that are wrecking our current institutions and provides us possible solutions that are cheaper and better. This is a book that will make you think and likely change how you invest in education for yourself and your loved ones."

–SRIKUMAR RAO, TED Speaker, former Columbia professor, and author
of *Happiness at Work: Be Resilient, Motivated, and Successful - No Matter What*

"Whether you're a lifelong learner or passionate expert, *Leveraged Learning* will take you on a journey from the failures of our current system, through to a bright and exciting future for education and give you the tools to be a part of it."

–GREG SMITH, Founder and CEO of Thinkific

"Forget about four-year degrees and decades (or more) of debt. Stop what you are doing and read *Leveraged Learning*; it clearly lays out the future of education for students, employers and lifetime learners."

–JOHN RUHLIN, CEO of the Ruhlin Group, best-selling author of *Giftology*

"What if modern education was more about engaging curiosity instead of memorizing useless factoids? In this well-argued book, Danny Iny offers an insightful look into how we can (and must) transform the way we learn today. It starts with rethinking what we need to know and reimagining who we choose to teach it to us. Read this book to help you understand what it takes to do both."

–ROHIT BHARGAVA, adjunct professor at Georgetown University,
and *Wall Street Journal* best-selling author of *Non-Obvious*

"Danny offers a clear view into the present education crisis. He then leads us into a future where a new way of learning can transform the education crisis into humanity's greatest opportunity."

—CHRIS BADGETT, CEO of LifterLMS

"Many people talk about the uselessness and cost of degrees unused but no one has laid out as cogent an argument for a meaningful alternative for achieving true learning that best serves the student. Best of all, students won't be in debt until they are 40 or longer and they'll have the education they need for the purpose it will serve, just when they need it most."

—MICHAEL PORT, *NY Times, WSJ* best-selling author of *Steal the Show*

"This is a book that schools will hate and employers will love. Say goodbye to expensive and often useless degrees. (Be honest, how many people do you know who work in the field related to their degree? I don't know many.) Danny Iny presents a well-defined argument for how education has failed both students and employers and exactly how it not only needs to, but will, change. Say goodbye to 20 years of debt for classes and degrees you'll never use after the classroom and say hello to education the way it should be: precise, practical, and profitable."

—ANKUR NAGPAL, CEO of Teachable

"The conversation around education in these times is an important, nuanced one. Danny's book is full of interesting ideas, examples and is valuable for anyone navigating the world of learning and education."

—UJ RAMDAS, co-founder of Intelligent Change and
co-creator of *The Five Minute Journal*

"Most forms of traditional education are expensive, and they are failing their students, which is creating a significant demand for non-traditional education channels. In this excellent book, Danny Iny shows us how we can provide a more enriching experience for our students that will translate into more results for them, and more of an impact they will have on the world."

–DEREK COBURN, author of *Networking Is Not Working*

"Danny Iny says that in a world of broken education, we all lose. I couldn't agree more. I just wish there had been a Danny trying to fix the world in this way when education was failing me. But I'm grateful that he's helping to build a better future for my children."

–SEAN PLATT, CEO of Sterling and Stone,
and best-selling author of *Write. Publish. Repeat.*

"Iny is the foremost expert in online education and one who does it ethically and without sleaze. With *Leveraged Learning,* he has taken his real-world experience in growing his own online education business and helping entrepreneurs like me, and distilled it into a book that will help other entrepreneurs and those who have a lifelong learning passion. I cannot recommend it more highly."

–GINI DIETRICH, CEO of Arment Dietrich and
founder and author of *Spin Sucks*

"This book is a must-read for anyone who wants to thrive in today's highly competitive job market."

–MICHAEL VELTRI, Leadership Expert and best-selling author
of *The Mushin Way to Peak Performance*

"We live in an accelerated age that requires business to continually reinvent itself to remain viable and profitable. Yet, as Danny Iny explains in *Leveraged Learning*, our outmoded post-secondary educational system is not only inadequately preparing us to effectively execute in these realms, but leaving learners (ourselves and our children!) saddled with whopping debt from which they may never fully recover. A true visionary, Iny lays out a practical, effective and much needed solution that will empower students to thrive and prosper, and employers to find a workforce with the critical skills, abilities and emotional intelligence vital to succeed. This book is a game changer whose time has come."

–DIANE BOLDEN, President of Synchronistics,

and author of *The Pinocchio Principle*

"At the same time as the old mass education system is becoming more expensive, a new opportunity has arisen to unbundle education: from one and done to lifelong learning and from made for everyone to made for you. *Leveraged Learning* shows why this is happening and how you can take advantage of it."

–TAYLOR PEARSON, author of *The End of Jobs*

LEVERAGED
Learning

HOW THE DISRUPTION OF EDUCATION

HELPS LIFELONG LEARNERS AND

EXPERTS WITH SOMETHING TO TEACH

Danny Iny

IDEAPRESS
PUBLISHING

COPYRIGHT © 2018 BY DANNY INY

All rights reserved.

Published in the United States by Ideapress Publishing.

IDEAPRESS PUBLISHING | WWW.IDEAPRESSPUBLISHING.COM

All trademarks are the property of their respective companies.

ILLUSTRATION BY: CATHY HUTCHISON

Cataloging-in-Publication Data is on file with the Library of Congress.

ISBN: 978-1-940858-69-2

PROUDLY PRINTED IN THE UNITED STATES OF AMERICA
BY SELBY MARKETING ASSOCIATES

SPECIAL SALES

Ideapress Books are available at a special discount for bulk purchases for sales promotions and premiums, or for use in corporate training programs. Special editions, including personalized covers, a custom foreword, corporate imprints and bonus content are also available.

William Butler Yeats famously said that education is
not the filling of a pail, but rather the lighting
of a fire, and I couldn't agree more.

This book is for my loving parents,
Ruthy and Mayer, who passed me this wonderful torch.

For my wonderful wife, Bhoomi, who carries it with me.

And my two amazing children,
Priya and Micah, for whom we proudly bear it.

Table of Contents

"I NEVER LET SCHOOL GET IN THE WAY OF MY EDUCATION."

If you do a generic search on my name, this is the quote most often attributed to me. I have no idea why. I, obviously, said it at some point from some keynote presentation stage (or some tweet), somewhere. It has grown with me over the years, and like all good things on Instagram, every few months, it sprouts back up in some other way. And I'm forced to (kindly) remind everyone that these words were spoken by Grant Allen and Mark Twain more than a century before they came out of my mouth. Still, it stands as a fairly correct statement about my stance on formal education and the current way that educational institutions are run.

I sucked at school (both elementary and secondary). I'd start off my early mornings with pangs of anxiety that manifested itself into stomach aches. I'd struggle to pay attention in class. I was often caught day-dreaming. I just wanted out. It wasn't for me. In grade four or five, I remember the English teacher calling my mother at home, because I was not reading the book that was assigned to the class. If memory serves, the class was instructed to read John Steinbeck's *Of Mice and Men*. I didn't like it. So, I dug around and set my eyes on J.D. Salinger's *The Catcher in The Rye*. The English teacher would have none of it. My mother came to my defense. "At least," she told the teacher, "he's reading something meaningful." I was an avid comic book reader (still am!), and I think her response was simply out of shock that I wasn't caught reading *X-Men* or *Iron Man*, when I should have been reading the classics. History's a funny thing. I think that we could all agree that *X-Men* and *Iron Man* are, indeed, classics as well.

I had every intention of scraping through with a degree (that started) in Philosophy. I had no idea what I would do with said degree, but it made a ton of sense at the time. I figured, that this was one of the few degrees where all you had to do was be alone, read and write. Sounded perfect. It was aligned with my personality. If you are an introvert you do things very differently. You learn very differently. In fact, it's not just introverts. We all learn in very different ways. Education is impacted by age, gender, geography, and everything else that you can imagine. We tend to forget that formal education was basically established as a buffer. This buffer would keep children out of the workforce but would—at the time—teach them as if they were already some kind of cog in an assembly line. Maybe that's not fact-based history, but it sure is how I philosophically think about school. Take boys and girls of the same age, line them up in desks, have them memorize and read, and then figure out at the end of the day who is succeeding and who is falling behind. Uch. The pangs and stomach aches are raging back.

Back to college. My first year of post-secondary education was a bit of a blur. At the time, I was already publishing a rock music magazine. It was a full-time-plus job, and I was loving it. For context, if you've ever seen the movie, *Almost Famous,* that was (basically) my life. I was seventeen when I landed my first professional (read: paid) job as a journalist. I interviewed Tommy Lee from Mötley Crüe and—as I like to joke—it was all downhill from there. My days consisted of organizing interviews with musicians, selling ads for the magazine, ensuring that the printer was ready for the next issue, speaking to the magazine distributors, graphic designer, dealing with my business partner and more. At night, you could usually find me at a show, concert, or event. How was I supposed to fulfill this rock n' roll dream (and proper entrepreneurial venture) while also completing a college degree?

I was drowning. I was failing. And, I didn't want to break my parents' hearts. It was time for a sit down with them. After a short conversation with my parents, my mother ended it with the wisdom of Solomon. I'm paraphrasing here, but her comment was something akin to: "You can always go back to school, but you will only get this one shot to see this music magazine business to its fullest potential." We agreed that if music magazine publishing didn't work out, I would go back to school. I dropped out the next day. I never went back.

Around that same time, I got back into martial arts (I had dabbled with Kung Fu during my early high school years). I took my training very seriously on this go around. This was not a traditional martial art, but a modern system developed for close quarter combatives (aka Street Fighting) that was taught by Tony Blauer. Tony is still a close friend, but he moved on from developing his self defense system to become one of the world's leading close quarter combatives instructors in the world. Along with being a human deadly weapon and my coach, he was an avid reader. He believed that fights were 90 percent psychological and 10 percent physical. This meant a lot of studying and reading to understand humans and human nature. His office (and home) was wall-to-wall books. This is the classic Zen thinking, right? Be the empty glass. Always be the student. Always be learning. I'd glance through his extensive book collection and treated it like a personal library (with his permission). Around the same time, one of my employers passed me a Tom Peters' book, *The Project 50*. I dismissed it. Candidly, I thought that I was done with business books or text books or any books that seemed like "education." When I read books like *The Project 50* or Dan Millman's *Way of the Peaceful Warrior*, my life changed. Wait, business books don't have to be boring? Why didn't I get that memo?!

Books are education. Books are a huge part of my life. What about yours? And it's not just books. Around this time the Internet was coming online. It was a jaw-dropping and life-changing experience for me. More stuff to read and learn from (mostly free!). Being a part of this online revolution has changed my life in every way imaginable. For the past twenty years, I've been watching this space move from a world of online articles to hyper-in-depth (and innovative) ways that everyone (including you) can learn from.

School is no longer about degrees or classrooms. Just today, I was in the park and taking in a glorious summer day with some other local families. A high-powered investor started asking me about blockchain... and what it all means. This individual wanted to know where she could go to learn more about it. YouTube? Skillshare? Read Don (and Alex) Tapscott's book, *Blockchain Revolution*? Listen to a myriad of podcasts on the subject? Sign up to some respected industry newsletters? Attend a conference? There's always some way to learn, but you can only learn if you commit to your own education.

The choice is yours. This book is your guide. Danny has put together a fascinating look at what "learning" really means today... and going forward. This book gave me pause. I started tracking all of the many ways that I seek out knowledge, education, a chance to be the student and grow in my own professional journey. And what I learned is there are many fantastic teachers out there in all kinds of interesting areas of study. It's just a matter of seeking them out, taking their courses and applying the material (which is the hardest part).

So as a learner, as an educator, and as a business leader... where should you begin? Start with this book. Then just start. Pick up a book, subscribe to a podcast, take an online course (and if you don't know where to find one, just post about it on Facebook or Twitter or ask Danny). Times have changed, and the world's knowledge is all around us. You no longer need to be accepted into a program by a college to take on learning, and that means college degrees aren't the signal to employers that they used to be. Can't get that Harvard MBA that everyone is talking about? Why not take Seth Godin's altMBA (and tell me which one is creating is the best leaders for tomorrow)?

Don't let school get in the way of your education.

Mitch Joel, Founder of Six Pixels Group
Author of *Six Pixels of Separation* and *CTRL ALT Delete*
July 2018 | Montreal, Canada

THE STORY OF PROGRESS (AND EDUCATION)

W HAT IS an aardvark? When was the moon landing? Where is Mount Vesuvius?

When I was a child, I would look for answers to these questions in the *World Book Encyclopedia*. Complete with red leather binding and gold leaf, it was one of my family's prized possessions. I would pull the appropriate volume off the shelf, flip through the pages in hopes that there was an entry, and read through it looking for the tidbit of information that I needed.

By the standards of the 80s and 90s, that *World Book Encyclopedia* was a wonderful resource, but in today's world of Google, Siri, Wikipedia, and the host of other tools clamoring to provide you with instant answers, well... my trusty *World Book* falls pitifully short.

This new world of technology-aided omniscience is so pervasive that it has completely changed our expectations around what is and isn't reasonable. We're past the point of awe or wonder, and even past the point of really appreciating our pocket-sized oracles. Now we just expect it, and even a second of buffering delay, or the occasional question that stumps Siri, leads to bemusement and annoyance.

This, my friend, is the story of progress.

THE STORY OF PROGRESS, FROM "AMAZING!" TO "ARE YOU FREAKING KIDDING ME?!"

It begins with a change that allows us to accomplish what previously was relegated to fantasy or science fiction. Think of the Wright Brothers proving that powered human flight was possible in 1903, Neil Armstrong landing on the moon in 1969, or the sequencing of the human genome at the start of the current century.

That sense of wonder doesn't last long. We adapt, and soon marvel is replaced with appreciation and desire. It's no longer impossible... it's just the best available, and—to the extent that we can afford it, of course—we want it! This was commercial air travel around the time of the First World War, personal computing in the late 70s and early 80s, cell phones in the 90s, and electric cars over the past decade—doing double duty as great wonders of technology and convenience, and great symbols of luxury and status.

Progress continues its inexorable march forward. What was "best in class" gradually becomes the baseline of "good" service. We take it for granted as table stakes, and notice it only by its absence. Good examples include anything that we think of as a utility, like electricity, indoor plumbing, phone and cellular service, and basic Internet access. We don't marvel at a home complete with electricity and indoor plumbing, but we fume when our toilets back up, or we can't run an appliance without blowing a fuse.

Eventually, what was once new and shiny becomes old and lackluster. These are the things that are still with us even though they really shouldn't be, that elicit reactions of, "Really? Are you freaking kidding me?!" Whether it's obtuse government bureaucracy, hotels that charge $15 a day for Internet access, or those motion-activated faucets in airport bathrooms that can't seem to tell when your hands wave in front of them... they exist only because nobody has gotten around to fixing or replacing them, and we all know it's just a matter of time.

This is the story of progress, and also the story of education.

THE RISE AND FALL OF MODERN EDUCATION

Modern education dates as far back as the eleventh and twelfth centuries in Europe[1] and the seventeenth and eighteenth centuries in North America.[2] Almost everything about education has changed since those days, from the diversity of those consuming it (including men and women of all races and social strata) to the range of institutions providing it (not just the thousands of accredited universities around the world, but also K-12 education, continuing and executive education, alternative education, online courses, and more).

But the most important thing has remained constant: the promise and expectation of a better and more successful life upon graduation. Whether it was the very first official diploma awarded by Harvard University in 1813, a modern-day undergraduate, graduate, or post-graduate degree from an accredited university, or the slew of alternative and supplemental options that have emerged in recent decades, the core premise that justifies your enrollment (and their existence!) is that the trade of your time and money for their experience and certification will leave you smarter, wealthier, happier, or otherwise better than you were when they found you.

As measured against that benchmark, education has had a pretty good run. Once just for wealthy aristocratic elites, the twentieth century saw a surge in the number of people aspiring to the solid career and comfortable middle-class life that a university diploma offered. And for a while it delivered, and then some. A university degree, the archetype of modern education, was the golden ticket to success. If you were so lucky as to have the opportunity to get one, you knew that the lifetime benefits would outweigh the cost of money and time by orders of magnitude.

That was true for a long time, but somewhere during the shift from the twentieth century to the twenty-first, things started to change.

EDUCATION ISN'T KEEPING UP

Part of it was education's inability to keep up with the rapidly changing world for which it purports to prepare us; many of the hottest jobs of today didn't exist as recently as 15 years ago.[3] Another part of it was simple ubiquity undermining differentiation; if you're the only job applicant with a university degree, it gives you a huge advantage, but if every applicant has the same degree, it doesn't help you all that much. For these and other reasons that we'll explore, conventional education simply isn't the path to gainful employment that it once was; as of this writing the majority (yes, the majority!) of recent college graduates are either unemployed or underemployed,[4] and of those who do land jobs, only about a quarter find work in their fields of study![5]

Conventional education simply isn't the path to gainful employment that it once was.

These disappointing returns are set against the rapidly rising cost of education, and the correspondingly crippling debt that graduates must carry. As of this writing, graduating university students in America carry an average debt of $30,100,[6] which doesn't even account for the opportunity cost of going to school and not working full time.

So take the meager returns of modern education, add the soul-crushing debt carried by its graduates, and compound it with the projections that by the end of the next decade college tuition will grow to well over six figures per year,[7] and the only reasonable response is: "Really? Are you freaking kidding me?!"

You want me to trade $30k and 4 years of my life to most likely be unemployed? **Are you freaking kidding me?!**

IT'S NOT JUST A COLLEGE PROBLEM...
IT'S A LIFE PROBLEM

That college costs too much and delivers too little is a problem on many levels... but this is about more than just college. This runs deeper, to the goal of success and upward mobility that college is expected to serve. As recently as a few decades ago, there was a reliable formula for achieving those things in the developed world: As long as you work hard and get an education, you'll be just fine.

But increasingly, that isn't the case. While it's true that under-graduate and graduate degree holders earn substantially more than their peers on average, if you take Ivy League and other top schools out of the equation,[8] as well as a limited set of vocation-granting degree programs[9] (think engineering, computer science, medicine, etc.), the disparity is much smaller. The data are further skewed because college graduates tend to be concentrated in major population centers, where the cost of living (and therefore wages) is higher, and the large student debt burden drives a disproportionate percentage of graduates to more lucrative but perhaps less desirable fields like consulting and investment banking—which is why so many enter these fields only to burn out of them within a few short years. On top of all that, most post-college earning data are collected by voluntary self-reporting, which skews toward the graduates who are doing well and want to talk about it!

As a society, we think of a university diploma as the ticket to gainful employment, but that isn't supported by the data. If you adjust for all these factors, much of the difference in lifetime earnings disappears. This is surprising to many, whose impressions of the return on a university investment was formed decades ago. Things have changed since then, and the perception of a degree as prerequisite for entering the job market is simply no longer accurate. And weighed against the rapidly increasing cost, it doesn't take a financial genius to realize that it just isn't worth it.

So if the modern college diploma isn't the golden ticket to the good life... then what is? A slew of educational options have emerged in recent decades. Some attempt to replace college altogether, some attempt to bridge the gap between a college degree and meaningful employment, and some are intended as supplements to a traditional educational path. Here's a sampling of the things that are available for the modern learner to choose from:

- Repackaged university courses from companies like The Great Courses or on free massive open online courses (MOOCs) like Coursera and the Harvard/MIT collaboration edX.

- Intensive coding bootcamps at outfits like General Assembly.

- Continuing or executive education programs offered by universities and private institutions.

- Recreational courses offered at community centers.

- For-profit colleges of dubious credibility and standing.

- Courses from celebrity instructors on sites like CreativeLive and MasterClass.

- Corporate internal training centers and "universities."

- Self-study e-learning programs, apps, and software.

- Supplemental education videos on sites ranging from YouTube to Khan Academy.

- Online video courses presented by individual experts on teaching marketplaces such as Udemy and Udacity, or privately on their own platforms.

The list goes on and on... and on. But what has come of all these options?

Overall, the results are patchy and disappointing, but there are bright spots, which we'll explore in this book. Taken as a whole, though, the landscape of education is fragmented, ineffective, and overpriced; by and large, people are paying far too much for far too little. The broken university system is a prominent part of the problem, because it represents close to half of the $4+ trillion global education market.[10] But it's the entire market that's broken, not just college.

Fundamentally, we no longer have a place that we can reliably go to become valuable to (and valued by) the rest of society. That hurts so many of us, in so many different ways.

IN A WORLD OF BROKEN EDUCATION, WE ALL LOSE

The current dysfunction of education is so egregious because it hurts so many of us.

Most obviously, it hurts the graduates who find themselves with a degree that has practically no market value, forced to make ends meet as Starbucks baristas or Uber drivers.

> We no longer have a place that we can reliably go to become valuable to (and valued by) the rest of society.

It hurts the bearers of a combined $1.4 trillion of student debt.[11] For those keeping score, that's more than credit card debt... and unlike credit card debt, you can't even declare bankruptcy and free yourself of the potentially lifelong consequences of a bad decision you might have made as a teenager.

It hurts the employers who are starved for talent. Education hasn't prepared job seekers with the skills to fill more than six million open jobs in the United States alone, even as almost seven million Americans are unemployed and looking for work.[12]

It hurts the learners who seek alternatives. They waste enormous amounts of time and money bouncing between a host of imperfect options like MOOC programs with completion rates that max out at 15 percent,[13] overpriced continuing education programs offered by universities, and courses provided by private instructors of varying quality.

And it hurts educators and learning professionals. They labor heroically to brighten their students' futures, but often that their best efforts can't overcome the inertia and challenge of the systems in which they operate.

We all hurt from the broken nature of modern education, that no longer prepares us for success. And we all need a solution that is more than just a band-aid.

Thankfully, such a solution exists. That's what this book is about.

EDUCATION THAT WORKS

Before we consider the how of a solution, we need to know the what.

"Education that works" could mean any number of different things to any number of different people. Is it about certificates, degrees, and diplomas? Alumni networks and student life? Student experience and satisfaction? Courses and curricula? Competencies and learning objectives? Job prospects and financial return on investment?

For our purposes, "education" and "learning" will be used somewhat interchangeably to refer to the designed experiences that are meant to act as a short-cut to achieving whatever job prospects, financial rewards, upward mobility, social contribution, and personal fulfillment we might aspire to. The short-cut quality is important; if the educational experience doesn't reduce the time, money, or risk that it takes to get to where we want to go, then we're better off without it!

And what does it mean for education to "work"? Just that these outcomes be delivered reliably. That means for most or all students, and certainly not just for a minority or the outliers. It's not enough to say that some students succeed because they go to exceptional schools. Some people are exceptionally successful in spite of their education, or some find success through alternative paths like self-directed learning or entrepreneurship. When the fringes and outliers are the only ones achieving success, they do so in spite of the system rather than because of it.

We can't be (and aren't) satisfied with the old quip about education being the transfer of ideas from the teacher's notes to the student's notes, without passing through the head of either. Yes, we must impart knowledge and corresponding skills. That's a great start, but only one of the three key drivers that empower us to succeed. We must also impart the practice of developing meaningful insight, and support the balance of emotions and habits of fortitude that are needed to succeed through education, and the rest of life.

All of this must be done cost-effectively, too—meaning without breaking the bank, saddling anyone with back-breaking debt, or otherwise requiring an investment that simply isn't justified by the promised outcomes or the process it takes to deliver them.

That we should have (and have access to) an education that works might seem like a self-evident no-brainer, except that it is so frustratingly far from the world in which we now live.

So to arrive at an education that works, we have quite a lot to explore...

WHAT'S INSIDE THIS BOOK

This book is written for two types of people: the lifelong learners who consume education—and I'll argue that lifelong learning is less a matter of passion or recreation and more a simple requirement of relevance in this modern age—and also for the educators and learning professionals who work hard to provide it. And of course, many of us fall into both categories!

Our first task, which we'll undertake in the first half of this book, is to understand why education isn't working, and what needs to change. We'll explore this in five chapters:

1. **Why Modern Education Is Ineffective, Overpriced, and Ubiquitous** – This has as much to do with signals and bubbles as it does with the substance of that education, with frightening implications for degree-issuing institutions and their graduates.

2. **Education for the Age of Acceleration** – Exploring how our world is changing (think artificial intelligence, automation, intelligent appliances, and driverless cars), and what education must offer in order for us to stay relevant.

3. **The Changing Landscape of Learning** – Here we'll explore the four major transitions that are changing almost everything about the way we consume education.

4. **Economics of the New Education** – This exploration will get us to the root of why today's higher education is hamstrung by money, and where we can expect education to come from in the future.

5. **Learning from the Experts** – Finally, we explore the economics and educational requirements that lead us to the unlikely source of continuing education in the modern world.

Having firmly established exactly why the education of yesterday can't prepare us for the world of tomorrow, we'll roll up our sleeves and dig into what it will take to get it right. This begins with the art and science of human learning: what it entails, how it works, where it shines, and why it sometimes breaks down. Then we'll focus on the matters that are especially relevant to the creators and purveyors of education:

6. **Knowledge: Making It Easy For People to Learn** – This is all about memory and skill, and we'll explore why it can be so fickle and elusive, and how to accelerate and shortcut the process.

7. **Insight: Where Critical Thinking Meets Creativity** – We'll explore what insight is, why it is so elusive, and how to cultivate it.

8. **Fortitude: How the Tough Keep Going When the Going Gets Tough** – This is the hidden ingredient that keeps the tough going when the going gets tough. We'll explore why learning short-circuits for so many people, and what it takes to create a better script and outcome.

9. **Designing Great Courses** – Here we'll shift gears from the art and science of learning to a practical process for building courses that serve the needs of modern learners.

10. **The Six Layers of Leveraged Learning** – These are the pieces that go into building a world-class learning experience, from the content that you'll cover, to the success behaviors that you'll instill, the way that you'll deliver, the user experience that you'll create, and the accountability and support that you'll provide.

So yes, I'm hoping to do quite a lot with this book! And like any ambitious endeavor, it deserves a disclaimer or two.

DIRECTIONALLY CORRECT
(IS BETTER THAN PERFECTLY ACCURATE)

Let's start by being upfront about the fact that each of the many topics I just mentioned is broad, rich, and substantial, so much that every chapter could easily be expanded to an entire book—or several!

But this isn't that sort of book (or series). I'm not an academic, a researcher, or a journalist. I'm an educator and an entrepreneur who's had a lifelong love-hate relationship with education. I dropped out of high school, and went back to earn a graduate degree from a top school. I built an education company—not because of my degree, but rather in spite of it. And I've built a career on designing education that makes a real difference in the lives of my students. This book draws on the lessons that I've learned along the way. And while this book is well researched, its focus is pragmatic rather than scholarly, designed to help you move in the right direction now, by choosing directionally correct, useful, and immediacy over perfectly accurate, academic, and unavailable information for several more years.

For that reason, this book addresses the world of education with a fairly broad brush. Higher education will receive a good deal of attention, along with executive and continuing adult education, vocational training, independently provided in-person and online courses, and everything in between. Although the focus of this book isn't K-12 education (both because it isn't my expertise and because overabundant regulation makes it extra hard to do anything about influence), I'll include the lessons that we might extract from what we know about how children learn.

You might find that at least some of this book feels a bit U.S.-centric. I know that this might rankle if you're from another part of the world (which, hailing from Montreal, Canada, I am). That U.S.-centricity is just a function of a preponderance of available data as well as a cost and incentive structure around education that makes the American system an especially unsustainable leading indicator of changes that will come to the rest of the world. Put simply, while the price of education is particularly high in the United States, the opportunity cost of education is disproportionate to its value throughout the modern world.

Science fiction author William Ford Gibson famously said, "The future is already here, it's just not evenly distributed." As such, while everything I will share is researched and true, it is bound to be more true in some contexts and for some people than others. As such, it doesn't matter whether the assertions that I make are absolutely true in all cases, but rather whether they substantially more true than they were five or ten years ago, and whether they are likely to be even more true five or ten years from now. In other words, whether my arguments are directionally correct. Experience suggests that this is the case, and it follows that ignoring this perspective will lead to good money and time thrown after bad for all who consume education, and misdirected efforts and lost opportunities for those who seek to provide it.

So please read with an eye toward how these ideas might matter in your context, as opposed to why you might disagree. There's a good chance that this book will challenge some things that you've believed strongly for a long time. Thanks in advance, and happy trails!

PART 1

Why We Need Leveraged Learning

(Why Education Isn't Working,

and What Needs to Change)

CHAPTER 1

Why Modern Education is Ineffective, Overpriced, and Ubiquitous

W HEN YOU'RE in a new city, how do you choose a place to dine out? If you have the time, money, and inclination, you could spend weeks, or even months wandering the streets, sampling the food, and developing an encyclopedic knowledge of the local restaurant scene. But what if that isn't practical? What if you've got an important dinner meeting that needs a venue in a hurry, and you can't afford to make the wrong choice? In that case, you need a shortcut, so you turn to a review site like Yelp or Zagat. Their reviews and star ratings are signals of value, and we rely on them to make critical restaurant decisions.

Human psychology is hard-wired to rely on signals—not only with our dining habits, but with every area of life. Should I trust you when you tell me it's okay to cross the street? Should I take your advice about how to treat a stubborn headache? Answering these questions gets a lot easier if you're wearing a police officer's uniform or doctor's lab coat, respectively.

While signals can sometimes be manipulated, by and large they serve us well. After all, wearing a police uniform is a privilege granted only to those who have undergone police training and shoulder the responsibility to serve and protect. And while anyone could secure a doctor's lab coat, the presumption is that those wearing one went to medical school, paid their dues, and took an oath to do no harm. The restaurant reviews, too, are presumably a reflection of the real quality of the food, service, and dining experience at the establishments in question.

Signals are the shortcuts, heuristics, and rules of thumb that enable us to make good decisions in the multitude of instances where it is impractical or cost-prohibitive to undertake our own thorough investigation of substance.

So what does all this have to do with education? Simple: Education, like the restaurant reviews, police officer's uniform, and doctor's lab coat, is a signal.

THE EMERGENCE OF SIGNALS, AND SUBSTANCE OF EDUCATION

Just because something is a signal, doesn't mean it has no inherent value. Signals emerge from substance. Restaurants served great food before the reviews said they did, brave men and women vowed to uphold the law before they were recognized with a uniform or badge, and healers toiled to serve the wellness of their communities before they wore white lab coats.

Signals emerge from substance.

The same is true of education and degrees. First there was a need for people who possessed knowledge and skill, and then teachers and institutions set out to provide it. The degree certifying the knowledge of an institution's graduates came later. Harvard, for example, took 177 years from its founding to the issuance of its first diploma. Which makes sense; unless the name Harvard is already known and respected, why would anyone care that the university awarded you a diploma?

Which begs the question, what does the name "Harvard" signal? Or, for that matter, what is signified by any educational achievement that is respected in the modern world? The answer is plenty, starting with a level of knowledge and skill. If you have a degree in law, medicine, or engineering, for example, I probably can trust that you have a working knowledge of that field. And let's not forget that graduating from a college is a signal that you have what it takes to get into one, which implies a baseline of mental faculties, dedication, and willingness to work.

But that's just the beginning. A diploma also signals that you belong to the right club and are a part of the right networks. In addition, you have the financial wherewithal (through personal wealth, connections, or resourcefulness) to afford the experience, which historically has said a thing or two about your background and upbringing.

Diploma

I vouch that _John_ is smart, hard-working, well-to-do, from a good family, and also knows a thing or two about whatever he studied.

All this conveyed by a single piece of paper. No wonder education has been such a powerful key to the good life, or that so many people wanted it so badly! That desire has kicked the economics of supply and demand into full gear, driving the cost of education up, and up, and up to a place of utter unsustainability.

But the real issue isn't the absurdly high price of education—that's just an exacerbating factor. The real problem is that the signal's value has been eroding for some time.

HOW THE SIGNAL TURNED TO SMOKE

Signals can lose their meaning. What happens when a restaurant realizes how important online reviews are to their success? They do whatever it takes to get more and better reviews, of course! Smart restauranteurs will be inspired to improve their food and service, and unscrupulous ones may resort to questionable tactics like asking friends, family, or freelancers on Craigslist to post favorable reviews that bump up their score.

And what about the review site whose operators realize how hot the commodity of a favorable review has become? Do they introduce a new service of premium reviews, by which restaurants can pay to have dedicated reviewers dine and post a presumably favorable account of the experience? And if that works, would the cost of this service continue to rise? For a while, this would look like an overheated market, with people doing everything they can to get in on the action. But it's a recipe for disaster, because the signal that once was backed by substance has turned to smoke.

Signals are only as good as their predictive power to help you make good decisions. That power can be eroded by several things, starting with simple ubiquity; if every restaurant has a hundred five-star reviews, they stop helping you choose among them. And on Halloween, when the streets are filled with people wearing uniforms and wearing stethoscopes, you think twice before taking their directions. Similarly, only five percent of males born in 1900 held a college degree.[14] Back then, letters after your name on a resume were a great differentiator, but in today's world, where nearly 40 percent of working-age Americans hold college degrees,[15] the letters don't have quite the same effect. This is the source of academic inflation: the curious combination of degrees being prerequisites for more and more jobs, even as they are insufficient to succeed in those jobs.[16]

Even worse than ubiquity is a disconnection from substance. To continue the restaurant analogy, imagine a review site based on speed of service, in an era where public desire turns to a slow cooking and dining experience. The reviews may be accurate and meaningful in their context, but they are no longer relevant in the context of their audience. In exactly the same way, the working world of the present and future is simply out of alignment with the substance that education once signified.

THE DISCONNECTION OF SIGNAL FROM SUBSTANCE

Part of the reason is the lecture format that most colleges still employ, which isn't an effective structure for most students.[17] Part is the inertia created by accreditation, which can make it challenging to re-engineer curricula to reflect modern needs. Part is that most course developers and instructors aren't practitioners, so they don't even know what modern needs really are. Part is tenure, which allows academics to focus on their passion for particular topics rather than the areas that the market needs most. And a large part is that most university programs were designed either by and for academics, or in the case of MBA-type programs, by and for big business. Neither group is much like the small and mid-market businesses that make up the majority of our economies and job markets.

The working world of the present and future is simply out of alignment with the substance that education once signified.

This misalignment with the needs of our graduates as individuals and economy as a whole is especially true with the degrees that you don't specifically need for any job, but check the box of "requires an undergraduate degree," no matter how unrelated to the task at hand. These non-vocational degree programs, like liberal arts and even business degrees in the absence of a career track headed for accounting or consulting or investment banking, simply aren't designed to make their students valuable in the workplace. Using them to accomplish that objective is like using your shoe to hammer in a nail. It might work, but it's definitely not the best tool for the job. And employers know it.

In an annual survey by Express Employment conducted in April of 2017, employers were asked to rank twenty factors they consider when making hiring decisions. Consistent with the results of the past several years, education was ranked dead last.[18] This might be surprising, until you consider the 2005 adult literacy study by the U.S. Department of Education found that the majority of college graduates couldn't do things like compare and contrast viewpoints in two newspaper editorials, and 14 percent scored at the basic level of literacy, which is just good enough to read books written for elementary school children.[19]

"They might graduate, but they are failing to develop the higher-order cognitive skills that are widely assumed college students should master."

Similarly, New York University researchers Richard Arum and Josipa Roksa found that 45 percent of students showed "exceedingly small or empirically nonexistent" gains in critical thinking, complex reasoning, and written communication during their first two years of college, and 36 percent showed no improvement over the entire four years of their education: "They might graduate, but they are failing to develop the higher-order cognitive skills that are widely assumed college students should master."[20] Bryan Caplan, professor of economics at George Mason University, put it this way:

> Human capital purism advances a single explanation: education pays because education teaches lots of useful job skills. A tempting story… until you stare at what schools teach, what students learn, and what adults know. Then human capital purism looks not just overstated, but Orwellian. Most of what schools teach has no value in the labor market. Students fail to learn most of what they're taught. Adults forget most of what they learn. When you mention these awkward facts, educators speak to you of miracles: studying anything makes you better at everything. Never mind educational psychologists' century of research exposing these so-called miracles as soothing myths.[21]

This sad state of affairs is at least partially responsible for the unimpressive employment rates of recent graduates. In 2011, 50 percent of college graduates younger than twenty-five were jobless or underemployed, and those who were working were more likely to be waiters, waitresses, or bartenders than engineers, physicists, chemists, or mathematicians (100,000 versus 90,000).[22]

The ultimate vote of no confidence in the system of traditional education can be seen in the rise of in-house corporate learning centers. General Electric pioneered this approach in the 1950s with its GE University, and today there are nearly five thousand of them.[23] That's five thousand organizations whose core competence is not education, who think that the substance of modern education is so out of alignment with their needs that they would rather do it themselves!

> Incredibly, even as the value of the education signal has declined, its cost has continued to rise.

Conventional education no longer prepares us for the real world, or offer us the useful skills that we need to be successful. Employers know this, and the signal is quickly eroding. But incredibly, even as the value of the education signal has declined, its cost has continued to rise.

THE PRICE OF EDUCATION: TO INFINITY, AND BEYOND?

This trend has been quite some time in the making. For more than 30 years, higher education tuition has grown at double the rate of inflation.[24] Ryan Craig, author of *College Disrupted*, offers this comparison:

> Working at the minimum wage in the late 1970s, a typical student at a four-year college could pay her entire tuition by working 182 hours—a part-time summer job. In 2013, the same student at the same college at the present-day minimum wage would have to work over 991 hours (a full-time job for half the year) just to cover tuition while still finding additional resources to pay for living expenses (and finding the time to attend classes)![25]

Because most students don't have that kind of money, they take on debt, and lots of it. As of this writing, seven in ten university students graduate with an average debt of $30,100,[26] at an interest rate of 4.7 percent.[27] Given that it takes about 20 years on average to repay the debt, that raises the real cost of the debt to more than $46,000 and that doesn't even account for the opportunity cost of going to school and not working full time, which is estimated at another $54,000.[28] This last part is a crucial factor; whereas American education is notoriously and obscenely over-priced, one might argue that it's a different story in places like my native Canada (where education is an order of magnitude cheaper), or parts of Europe (where it is completely free). But the hard cost of education is only part of the equation. There's also the opportunity cost, which is substantial even if you live in a part of the world where higher education doesn't cost a dime.

This is unsustainable, increasingly harder to justify, and out of reach of many people who still aspire to achieve such a degree. Klaus Schwab, the founder and executive chairman of the World Economic Forum, states:

> Today, a middle class job no longer guarantees a middle-class lifestyle, and over the past 20 years, the four traditional attributes of middle-class status (education, health, pensions and house ownership) have performed worse than inflation. In the US and the UK, education is now priced as a luxury.[29]

And high as the price might be today, projections are that college tuition will grow to as high as $130,000 per year by the end of the next decade.[30] William Bowen, the president of Princeton University, explained that because it's a people-intensive industry and people have to keep pace with inflation, there are no productivity gains to be had in a university (unlike a manufacturing facility, for example), so we should expect those prices to continue to rise in perpetuity.[31]

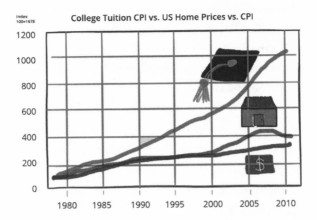

These figures are horrendous, but they're also unfairly optimistic because many of them assume an unrealistically timely graduation. In reality, only 20 percent of students entering a four-year bachelor's degree program graduate within four years.[32] Student debt gets wildly out of control as students continue past the four-year range, and many don't finish at all. While graduation rates at the top fifty schools approach 90 percent, overall graduation rates hover around 55 percent for four-year institutions and 29 percent for two-year colleges.[33] There are currently 31 million Americans, representing more than 20 percent of the workforce, who have some college credits but no completed degree.[34]

If you feel dumbstruck by this data, you're not alone. Anyone who is currently mid- or late-career will have "grown up" in a very, very different educational context. Just a few decades ago, the cost of education was a fraction of what it is now, and the benefits were substantial. But in just a few short decades, things have changed almost beyond recognition.

AREN'T DEGREES STILL TABLE STAKES?

Warren Buffett, known as the "Oracle of Omaha" is one of the most successful investors of all time. Famous for his adherence to value investing and personal frugality, he's grown a net worth of over $80 billion. This is the product of a lifelong investing career that began with his first stock purchase at age 11. To be sure, Buffett had a lot of things going for him in order to get to where he is today: instincts, vision, discipline, and probably a healthy dose of luck. And also one thing that every other investor on the planet has: money to invest. Not that having money automatically makes you a successful investor, but without any money you can't invest at all.

In the same way that money is table stakes for investing, many believe that a university degree has become table stakes for a career. Not that a degree will necessarily get you a good job, but that it's hard or impossible to get a good job without one. If this is true, then it doesn't really matter how bad the ROI is on a college education; if you need it, you need it. But do you really need it?

Warren Buffet's story is instructive. It's true that he needed money to invest, but he didn't need all that much. His first investment at age 11 was for a grand total of six shares of the oil company Cities Service; three for himself and three for his sister Doris, at the price of $38 a share. Similarly, while there is truth to the "degree as table stakes" argument, it is much more limited in scope than most people think.

Remember that signals only ever matter in the absence of better information. If I know you and have experience working with you and have seen that you can do a job well, I won't care where or if you went to school. It is only in the absence of that familiarity and knowledge that signals really matter. So the question isn't just one of "does the signal matter", but also "can I get around the signal?" How easy or difficult it is to do that depends on the size of the organization in question; as a rule of thumb, the bigger the organization the harder it is to find creative ways to connect with a hiring manager and make a good impression.

Simply by virtue of the number of people who apply to work at larger companies every day, they put up walls to keep resourceful applicants from bothering their staff, and use applicant tracking system (ATS) technologies to scan the abundance of resumes that they receive. This is a problem for job seekers, but how big of a problem? First, let's consider how much of the job market this actually reflects. Yes, cumbersome HR processes and ATS technologies are common in big business, but 51 percent of jobs come from small businesses, not big ones.[35] Given that a quarter of recruiters and talent managers don't use ATS technology,[36] that brings the percentage of overall jobs unaffected by these challenges up to over 63 percent. So actually there are a lot of good jobs that lacking a degree doesn't lock you out of.

But even when it comes to the big companies that do employ ATS technology, the systems can be gamed by formatting resumes in just the right way, or cleverly using certain keywords. (For example, most ATS systems can't tell the difference between "graduated with a Bachelor of Arts from Acme University" and "pursuing a Bachelor of Arts from Acme University." Just Google "how to write a resume that will beat the ATS" for more ideas.)

Most importantly, though, larger organizations are already moving away from the degree as a criteria for employment, as you'll see in later chapters. While ATS technologies will get eventually get better and smarter, the same is true of the companies that use them, which means they'll be screening for better things than a college degree. In short, no, degrees aren't the all-access pass to a career that universities like to pretend they are. The cost is exorbitant, the returns are meager, and the entire situation is completely unsustainable. So how much longer can it go on?

Degrees aren't the all-access pass to a career that universities like to pretend they are.

THE EDUCATION BUBBLE, AND THE HARD QUESTIONS IT RAISES

Economic bubbles are made up of two factors: simultaneously stagnant (or declining) value, and rising cost (including opportunity cost). The cost is clearly rising, and we've established that the value of traditional education is declining. Sooner or later, bubbles pop, but they don't always pop to dramatic effect, especially when so many are so invested in the current establishment, which is more true of education than almost anything else. As tech investor Peter Thiel explained,

"Education may be the only thing people still believe in in the United States. To question education is really dangerous. It is the absolute taboo. It's like telling the world there's no Santa Claus."[37]

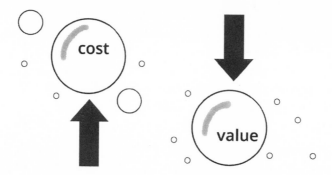

Some crashes are sharp, to the tune of a stock index losing a substantial portion of its value in a single day. Others are more gradual—less of a "pop," and more of a rapidly deflating balloon. The crash of education is likely to follow the latter pattern, and there's good reason to believe that it's already underway; during the past five years, higher education enrollment declined more than 6.5 percent.[38] That might not seem like much, but it's substantial and a sign of things to come.

That raises some difficult and uncomfortable questions: What are the implications for higher education institutions? What happens to the value of the degrees that universities have granted and will continue to grant? By extension, what happens to the holders of those degrees? And if university degrees lose their value, does that mean people won't go and we'll end up with an overall uneducated society?

Let's start by acknowledging that the Ivy League and other elite schools aren't going anywhere. Harvard's endowment will let them weather any storm. McGill's alumni network will continue to give its graduates a leg up. Oxford's industry connections will ensure its graduates get hired. For these schools, learning is actually a secondary concern when it comes to the value of the degree. As such any school will be just fine if it has some combination of a massive endowment that can weather storms, connections with key industry and celebrity professors, an elite brand reputation, and a strong and well-connected alumni network.

Community colleges can be expected to survive as well; their cost structure is very different, and they form a strong base for many students. Vocational training will be around for as long as the training does a good job of preparing its graduates to do the work, and that vocation continues to be a worthwhile and prosperous career choice. Some institutions of higher learning will persist as research sites and vocational training for academics. And there will always be a certain amount of demand for overpriced education from people who consume it as an expensive hobby.

WHY HIGHER EDUCATION IS GROUND ZERO FOR DISRUPTION

All of these represent less than 20 to 30 percent of the current educational establishment. The bulk of the rest—especially organizations with high fees and middling reputations—will face declining enrollment, and many will go the way of the dinosaur, because there are too many things about the way they work that don't make sense, as Todd Hixon articulated so well in his *Forbes* article titled "Higher Education Is Now Ground Zero for Disruption:"

- A residential, facilities-based approach that drives high fixed costs and requires students to reside away from home and job opportunities.

- Parallel development of standard curricula (e.g., Economics 101) by two thousand U.S. colleges and universities.

- Parallel delivery of standard curricula live on two thousand campuses.

- Relatively equal allocation of key resources (staff and student loans) to degrees in fields of study that are in demand in the economy, and those that are not. Fewer than 10 percent of U.S. bachelor-level graduates are in the highly demanded STEM (science, technology, engineering, and mathematics) fields.

- Cross-subsidization among teaching employment skills, liberal arts education, research, scholarship, and operating a vast country club. Essentially, the minority of stuff that people really want and value is subsidizing all the rest.

- Focus on the university degree as the credential, versus specific courses and skills accomplished.

- Little investment in the career success of graduates. This is not rocket science. University graduates lack basic skills like making presentations, using spreadsheets, business writing, and understanding what it means to be an employee of a business.[39]

Put simply, if an institution charges in the same range as Ivy League institutions but sports unimpressive graduation rates, middling post-graduation employment rates, and low starting salaries for the graduates who manage to find a job, the fact that they're easy to get into for people who want a college experience will no longer do the trick.

This could mean mergers, closures, or both, all of which are already happening in quite a few places, including Marylhurst University in Oregon, Wheelock College in Massachusetts, and St. Gregory's University in Oklahoma. It also might mean a shift in focus to more adult learners, who are a growing market.[40]

But wait, as wrongheaded as so much of what colleges today might be doing, can't they just fix it? Isn't there a scenario where they get their act together and get back on track? Sadly, the answer is probably not, partly because of economic reasons, but largely because current education is woefully out of step with the needs of the modern world in pretty much everything, from the curriculum itself, to the structure through which it is delivered, to the way it is packaged, to the incentives for changing and improving it (or not), to the outcomes that it does (or doesn't!) deliver.

So does that mean college is always, everywhere, and for everyone a bad idea? No, not quite. While most of the reasons given for attending college don't hold water, there are still some very good reasons to consider it.

GOOD AND BAD REASONS FOR GOING TO COLLEGE

In the early 1800s, a British aristocrat was craving a flavor he had tasted when stationed in India as Governor of Bengal. So he visited the chemist shop of John Lea and William Perrins, and asked them to prepare it. Lea and Perrins made an extra jar for themselves, but didn't like the concoction, and stored in the cellar. Some years later they gave it another taste, and found that age had made it delicious. Thus was born Worcestershire Sauce, by Lea and Perrins.[41]

Worcestershire's strong umami flavor is a great addition to some drinks, marinades, and sauces,[42] but use with care, because whereas you can almost never go wrong adding salt or lemon juice to a dish, Worcestershire sauce only mixes with very particular flavors. This is a good analogy for a college education—great in certain contexts, but not a good idea for most people. So what are the contexts in which a college degree still makes a ton of sense?

In pursuit of a specific vocation. If you want to be a doctor, lawyer, engineer, accountant, architect, nurse, or any other profession that requires specific training and a license, then traditional education is still the path that will get you there. Just make sure the vocation is as interesting to you as you expect it will be (job shadowing is great for this), and that it is as viable a career choice as you think it is (prospects in the legal industry, for example, are looking bleak, as we'll see in chapter 7).

If the college is selective. Of the many thousands of higher education institutions in the United States, only about two hundred of them are selective, meaning that they accept less than 50 percent of the students who apply. Those selective institutions are the ones whose degrees are most valuable, and signal the things that are truly valuable.

If you can comfortably afford it. Spending money that you have is very different from spending money that you don't—both because debt increases the real cost substantially, and because of the repayment burden that it creates. So if you can go to college without taking on debt—either because you or your family have lots of money in the bank, or because you can access scholarships—then the ROI math changes significantly.

If you can't count on the benefit of the doubt. A rare signal (like a degree when hardly anyone had one) tells us that its bearer is better than all those who don't have it. A common signal, on the other hand, tells us that its bearer is no worse than all those who do. This sort of signaling doesn't matter if you're the sort of person (typically a white male) that society is trained to give the benefit of the doubt; that you're no worse than everybody else is just taken for granted. But if society generally does not extend you that benefit of the doubt and you have to prove your worth on every occasion, a signal of "no worse than everyone else" carries more value—as is the sad reality for many women and minorities. This will of course change as the signal continues to erode, but it will probably hold value in this context for at least a few more years.

If any (or ideally several) of these three criteria are true, college might be a good idea. On the other hand, most of the reasons usually given in support of college don't make much sense at all, including...

As table stakes for entering the workforce, or to earn more money in your career. As we've seen in this chapter, neither of these goals is well served by a college education, though comparatively speaking, the impact is greater for women and minorities than for white men.

To find out what you want to do with your life. College is a very expensive and inefficient way of finding this out, and the volume of topics, ideas, and opportunities that you'll actually be exposed to is surprisingly limited. Much better to read widely, engage in some job shadowing, and secure internships or apprenticeships, as we'll explore in later chapters.

To become well-rounded. Taking a handful of electives as part of your degree doesn't make you well-rounded. At best, it makes you a bit eclectic. More importantly, if the goal is to be well-rounded, then spending a few dozen hours and a few hundred dollars on books or documentaries will take you farther than a much larger investment in college.

To learn about things that interest you. If you're genuinely interested in learning, you'll best be served by independently going deep on your topic of interest, and learning from the very best instructors in the world through their books and online courses.

In most cases, a traditional formal education just doesn't make sense. That doesn't mean, though, that we're headed for a future without education. On the contrary, an education that is well thought out and delivered has never been more important or necessary. In the next chapter, we'll explore what it will take for education to be relevant in the world that we're growing into, based on what it will take for *us* to be relevant in that world.

DID YOU GET ALL THAT? (LEARNING SELF-ASSESSMENT)

We've all been there: snapping out of a daze, we realize that we've driven all the way to our destination, but don't remember any of journey. Our experience and skill with driving and the specific route make it such that we can do it without any conscious attention. The same is true of other tasks that we've been doing for years, like perhaps cooking, gardening... or reading. I've definitely had the experience of curling up with a good book, being completely engrossed by the ideas between its covers, and then suddenly realizing that my mind had wandered. Without realizing it, I had gone through several pages, and didn't have the faintest idea of what they were about.

This is normal, and a problem that some authors address by simply repeating each big idea ten or fifteen times. I've opted for another solution: while endeavoring to be as concise as possible, I'll end each chapter with ten or fifteen questions that you can use to check your understanding of the topics that we just finished exploring. Feel free to use them as you see fit, test your understanding to help with encoding and recall, start conversations with interested friends and colleagues, or to skip over them completely and go straight to the next chapter. Here are the first set:

1. What are some examples of signals, and what are they useful for?

2. What is signified by a college diploma?

3. Why is the value of that signal not as strong as it used to be?

4. What is the source of "academic inflation"?

5. In the April 2017 survey by Express Employment, employers were asked to rank 20 factors they consider when hiring. Which factor ranked last?

6. In-house corporate learning centers, like GE University, are on the rise. What does tell us?

7. In the last 30 years, how has the growth of college tuition compared to inflation?

8. Why is the cost of education most likely to continue rising in perpetuity?

9. What good reasons to we have to believe that education is a bubble?

10. What kind of educational institutions will be most affected when the education bubble bursts?

11. What are some of the characteristics of educational establishments that are ripe for disruption?

12. What are the possible scenarios when the education bubble pops?

LIKE WHAT YOU READ, AND WANT TO GO DEEPER?

As I mentioned in the introduction, each chapter in this book could easily have been expanded to an entire book, or several. In case you're inclined to go deeper on the topics that I'll share with you, each chapter will conclude with a few recommended books for further reading. On the topic of the challenges of modern education, the recommendations are:

- Bryan Caplan's *The Case Against Education*
- Ryan Craig's *College Disrupted*
- Craig Brandon's *The Five Year Party*

For more information, including this entire book in digital format plus actionable conversation video guides at the end of each chapter, an expanded and up-to-date bibliography, and additional resources, visit LeveragedLearningBook.com

Education for the Age of Acceleration

W HEN ALDOUS HUXLEY published *Brave New World* in 1932, it was hailed as a masterpiece. His picture of a dystopian society more than six centuries into the future was mind-blowing, complete with humans manufactured in artificial wombs, babies indoctrinated into castes, and all pain eliminated by a drug called Soma.

Amid those frightening futuristic predictions were some that, from our vantage point, are mostly amusing and quaint. Take the elevator scene in chapter 4, for example. In Huxley's day, elevators were mechanical contraptions operated by liftmen, whose job was to maneuver the elevator to your destination by pulling the appropriate levers. Huxley realized that the idea of this being done by a human being so far into the future was laughable, so he imagined a suitably dystopian solution: a genetically engineered sub-human creature of the lowest caste.

You read that right. Huxley could imagine elaborate genetic engineering, but the idea of simply pushing a button and getting where you want to go eluded him. It seems obvious to us now, but Huxley was writing well before the electronic revolution, so there was no frame of reference for anything operated by a computer.

This is a common theme in science fiction; it may include a big idea for how things might be different, but the rest is imagined to remain

Star Trek, for all that it got right with its vision of a bold egalitarian future, still had women wearing miniskirts in space. strikingly the same. *The Jetsons*, for example, is essentially a depiction of family life in the 60s, with the addition of jetpacks, spaceships, and food pellets. *Star Trek*, for all that it got right with its vision of a bold egalitarian future, still had women wearing miniskirts in space. And while it was a big step forward to have an African-American woman on the bridge, let's not forget that her job was to answer the space telephone.

PREDICTIONS ABOUT THE FUTURE OF EDUCATION

I heard just this sort of prediction of the future at the 2018 conference of the Association for Talent Development. With 12,000 learning professionals attending from all around the world, and keynotes from the likes of President Barack Obama and management guru Marcus Buckingham, it's among the world's biggest conferences on the business of learning. On the morning of the first day, I joined a conference session about the future of education.

The experience was underwhelming, to say the least. The session began with dimmed lights and a video. For five minutes, we watched bombastic facts about the present and projections about the future flash on the screen:

"China will soon become the NUMBER ONE *English speaking country in the world, and India has more honors kids than America has kids."*

"The top 10 in-demand jobs in 2010 did not exist in 2004. We are currently preparing students for jobs that don't yet exist using technologies that haven't been invented in order to solve problems we don't even know are problems yet."

"If Facebook were a country it would be the third largest in the world. (behind China & India)."

"We are living in exponential times. There are 31 billion searches on Google every month. Today, the number of text messages sent and received everyday exceeds the total population of the planet."

"The amount of new technical information is doubling every two years. For students starting a four-year technical degree this means that half of what they learn in their first year of study will be outdated by their third year of study."

All these pronouncements were made against the backdrop of a chanting refrain, "right here, right now!" It was a slightly updated version of Karl Fisch and Scott McLeod's original *Shift Happens* video,[43] which I first watched in 2008—an ironic start to a presentation about the future! And it was all downhill from there, with discussions about the need for educators to use more technology, make the student's smartphone part of the learning experience, and leverage resources like TED Talks as part of lectures. Those are all good ideas, but in terms of thinking about and preparing for the future, it's a *Jetsons* level of prediction and imagination.

Lectures are among the least effective pedagogical devices known to man.

Worst of all, it was a lecture. Sure, there were some videos and a few "high five and discuss with the person sitting next to you" moments, but it was still a lecture. And lectures are among the least effective pedagogical devices known to man. That's one of the biggest ironies: that most every class I've taken on "cutting-edge adult learning" has been taught using all the modalities (lectures, trivial homework, facile tests) that *aren't* cutting-edge adult learning.

Finally, I gave up and walked out of the session. Never mind the *future* of education, this wasn't even an accurate picture of the *present* of education!

A BRAVE NEW WORLD (RIGHT HERE, RIGHT NOW!)

The conference presentation can be forgiven for being a little out of date and out of touch. They're good people who care deeply about their work, but the sad truth is that they're probably just a little too close to the problem.

There is one important insight about predicting the future in the video's refrain of "right here, right now." Imagining the distant future is very hard. As my colleague Rohit Bhargava, author of the *Non-Obvious* book series about predicting trends and winning the future explains, it's both easier and infinitely more useful to extrapolate from what's happening now than it is to make up what might happen later.

> The only way education can be sustainable and legitimate is to deliver an outcome that is meaningful in the present and future world.

As Kevin Carey argues in *The End of College*, the only way education can be sustainable and legitimate is to deliver an outcome that is meaningful in the present and future world.[44] But what will it take to do that? Joseph E. Aoun, president of Northeastern University, wisely wrote that "the existing model of higher education has yet to adapt to the seismic shifts rattling the foundations of the global economy."[45] So what are those changes?

It would be a cop-out to satisfy ourselves with an acknowledgement that we're all more digitally connected than we used to be, and therefore education needs to use more technology. That's *Jetsons*-level prediction, again, obvious (no kidding, we're using more technology), but neither insightful nor helpful. (The proliferation of technology in learning is much less about doing things on our phones and much more about the capability for a-synchronous and semi-synchronous just-in-time learning.)

We need to understand the seismic shifts that call for us to change not only *how* we teach, but also *what* we teach, in order for our students to be ready and relevant. What's happening right here, right now, that will make the world substantially different later?

SENSORS, CONNECTIVITY, AND ARTIFICIAL INTELLIGENCE... OH MY!

One of the hotter topics in the technology press in recent years is that of autonomous vehicles, also known as self-driving or driverless cars. The concept has been in various forms of research and development for decades, but in the past few years there's been a substantial acceleration (no pun intended), with hundreds of millions of miles of autonomous driving under the belts of leaders in the field,[46] like Google, Tesla, Uber, and Mobileye. Tech companies are not alone in this trend; automakers ranging from Audi to Volvo have also invested heavily in building a driverless experience.[47]

Whether driverless vehicles are a good thing or not is a matter of debate, with strong arguments on both sides. On the plus side, there's safety (more than 90 percent of traffic accidents are attributable to human error),[48] productivity (at an average of 26 minutes each way to work, five days a week, fifty weeks a year, that's a collective 3.4 million American person-years that could be redeployed),[49] and affordability (millions of people work in transportation,and even assuming an entry-level salary, they represent tens of billions of dollars of cost, which can be saved and passed on to consumers).[50] That brings us to the argument for why it's a bad thing. Transportation is one of the largest industries in the world, and automation is expected to lead to massive job loss.

What most pundits agree on is that it isn't a matter of *if*, but rather *when*. The more bullish might argue for commercial driverless cars on the road in just a few years, and the more bearish might think we're a decade or more away. My personal belief is that it probably will be closer to the latter, based on the maturity of technology, constraints of insurance and legislation, and a timeline for public willingness to get on board. Even in the most pessimistic perspectives, there's no question that when my children (born in 2015 and 2016) reach what we now call "driving age," they'll think of driving their own vehicles the same way we think of when our parents or grandparents would drive without seat belts or ride bicycles without helmets: "What do you mean, you drove your own car... that's so dangerous!"

BELLWETHER FOR THE AGE OF ACCELERATION

I'm excited to ride in a driverless vehicle, but what's most interesting for our purposes is the confluence of technologies that will make such a ride possible, and what they tell us about what our world is fast becoming. These technologies and changes have much broader implications than the automotive and transportation industries; they're the bellwethers of what Thomas Friedman calls the *Age of Acceleration*, which is the environment that modern education must prepare us for.

So let's consider these technologies, and their implications. Building a truly autonomous car takes a lot, including:

- **Sensors that can see and hear what is going on around the vehicle.** Check. We already have sensors that can replicate sight, hearing, touch, and taste, and smell is on the way. Not only does the technology exist, but also it's also small, cheap, and hardy enough that we can put sensors in almost anything, ranging from industrial equipment to the "connected cow," a network of sensors attached to every member of the herd that tracking all manner of data for purposes of improving herd management and milk production.[51]

- **Computers fast enough to process all that data.** Check. Fifty years ago, co-founder of Intel, famously originated Moore's Law, predicting that every couple of years processor speeds will double, and their prices will drop in half. This has held true for the past fifty years, despite frequent predictions of its impending demise, leading jaw-dropping (and jaw-droppingly affordable) processing speed and power. Case in point: In 1996 the U.S. government commissioned the ASCI Red, a supercomputer that was the size of a tennis court, cost $55 million, and could process more than a trillion calculations per second for complex simulations. It was the most powerful computer in the world until the year 2000,[52] but by 2008 ATI was selling a Radeon HD 3870 X2 graphics card with the same processing power for only $450.[53]

- **Knowledge of the geography and traffic around you, and software smart enough to make driving decisions.** Check. This has been around for a while and is used by millions, through services like Google Maps and Waze. Movements like open source and tools like application programming interfaces allow for software complexity to be abstracted away, which means that software developers don't have to understand the full complexity of existing software to build on it.

- **The ability to make smart decisions, learn, and improve, both for individual vehicles and an entire fleet.** Check. Complex rules-based software engines allow driverless vehicles to make complex driving decisions, similar to the technology that allowed IBM's *Deep Blue* computer to beat Garry Kasparov in 1996. Machine learning and artificial intelligence (AI) algorithms allow driverless vehicles to learn from their experience and get better—like the technology that Deep Mind's *AlphaGo* used to beat Lee Sedol in 2016,[54] and Carnegie Mellon's *Libratus* beat four top poker players in 2017.[55] But unlike any of those systems, driverless cars are all networked to one another, which means each of them learns the lessons from the experience of the entire fleet.

Driverless Cars

☑ Sensors
☑ Computing Speed
☑ Information
☑ The Ability to Learn

As wondrous and incredible (or scary) as all these advances may sound, none of them are science fiction. They all exist today, albeit more so in some places than others. They are already in the process of proliferating into every area of life. So what happens in a world where everything is aware of its state and surroundings, is connected to everything else, and is smart enough to make decisions? The implications for our economies and job markets are profound, which in turn changes the work that education needs to do in order to prepare us for it.

> As wondrous and incredible (or scary) as all these advances may sound, none of them are science fiction.

WHY AN OUNCE OF PREVENTION CAN BE A POUND OF LOST JOBS

Consider the faint "drip, drip, drip" that you might hear from a leaky pipe in your kitchen. If you catch it early, the fix is cheap and easy. If left to fester, the result can be messy and costly to remedy.

The same thing happens underground with municipal piping. A leak leads to the same "drip, drip, drip," but nobody can hear it. So the problem festers until it gets big and messy, at which point entire stretches of highway have to be dug up, at a cost in the range of $1 million per mile.[56] That is, unless a sensor attached to the pipe can tell you if there's a problem before it gets that far and exactly where to dig. And sensors on pipes are just one illustration of the many ways in which the artificial intelligence and automation technologies we just explored will disrupt the job market. As Martin Ford explained in *Rise of the Robots*, "...we are, in all likelihood, at the leading edge of an explosive wave of innovation that will ultimately produce robots geared toward nearly every conceivable commercial industrial, and consumer task."[57]

An ounce of prevention really can save a pound of cure, and that's great if you're the one paying to relieve the pain, but not so great if your livelihood comes from providing the cure. Just as a few hundred dollars' worth of sensors can save a few million dollars' worth of repairs down the road, the various technologies we're discussing create the potential for massive disruption to the employment market. Thomas Friedman describes four directions in which jobs will be pulled:

1. **Up:** You'll need increasing amounts of knowledge and skill to perform the same job. For example, automation of milking cow herds means that a herd manager will need computer and data analysis skills.

2. **Apart:** The skilled parts of a job will require even more skill and knowledge, while the unskilled parts will require even less. Continuing with the automated milking example, the milker will need more skill, but the manure shoveler will need less. The job probably will be performed by two people or even more likely, by one person and one machine.

3. **Out:** Outsourcing and automation will compete successfully for more jobs, and for bigger portions of jobs that still require humans. Given that computers and machines are stronger and faster than we are, and they don't get tired or make sloppy mistakes, it's a competition that humans aren't likely to win.

4. **Down:** As the world evolves, jobs, skills, and knowledge become obsolete at ever faster rates. As articulated in the *Shift Happens* video, "for students starting a four-year technical degree, this means that half of what they learn in their first year of study will be outdated by their third year of study."[58]

HEADED FOR DISRUPTION

In short, we're headed for a job market disruption the likes of which we've never seen before. A frequently quoted 2013 Oxford University white paper forecasts that 47 percent of jobs could be eliminated by smart technology during the next two decades, and a 2017 McKinsey & Company report predicts that 49 percent of the time we spend working (which translates to more than $2 trillion in annual wages in the United States alone) could be eliminated by current technology.[59] In consulting firm PWC's 2018 *Workforce of the Future* report, 37 percent of respondents were concerned about automation putting jobs at risk.[60] Some predictions are even more grim, as Joseph E. Aoun shares in his book *Robot-Proof*:

> We're headed for a job market disruption the likes of which we've never seen before.

> In late 2016, the White House's National Science and Technology Council's Committee on Technology released a report titled *Preparing for the Future of Artificial Intelligence*. In its heavily footnoted fifty-eight pages, the report offers policy recommendations for dealing with machines' imminent capacity to "reach and exceed human performance on more and more tasks." As the report ominously notes, "In a dystopian vision of this process, these super-intelligent machines would exceed the ability of humanity to understand or control. If computers could exert control over many critical systems, the result could be havoc, with humans no longer in control of their destiny at best and extinct at worst."[61]

So is this the end of the world as we know it? Should we grab our rifles and fill our bunkers with bottled water and canned goods? No, not quite.

What's coming qualifies as a serious disruption to the economy and labor market, but let's be real for a moment: These things have happened before. The classic example is when Edwin Budding invented the lawn mower in 1830. It doesn't sound like a big deal until you consider that it sparked an explosion of sports innovation, which led to the creation of the professional and codified sports industries. That's right: Professional football, baseball, soccer, and more owe their existence to what is now called the Budding Effect,[62] that is, the unexpected opportunities created when things change. In the case of professional sports, the simple fact of having even, level mowed fields opened up a cornucopia of possibilities that had yet to be imagined.

We can expect the same thing to happen in the convergence of "STEMpathy" work (where the technical skills of science, technology, engineering, and math meet the humanistic skills of empathy and connection), but it's hard to say exactly where. We just aren't good at seeing these changes coming, for the same reasons that Aldous Huxley couldn't predict an electronic elevator, and that *Star Trek* imagined women would wear miniskirts in space. We're not good at imagining the implications of the implications of the implications of things that change. But historically speaking, this has happened over, and over, and over again.

So if we know that the Budding Effect will bring lots of jobs and opportunity into our world... but we don't know what they are, and can't see them coming. But we aren't flying totally blind. We do have a sense of what category of challenges they're likely to fall into.

SIMPLE VS. COMPLICATED VS. COMPLEX

Computers are getting smarter every day, but that doesn't mean there aren't areas in which we're much better than they are and will remain so for the foreseeable future. However, our strength probably isn't in the areas that many of us might imagine. Our intuition is actually bad at assessing what is easy and what is difficult. A good illustration is this comic from KXCD, which can be found online at https://xkcd.com/936/:

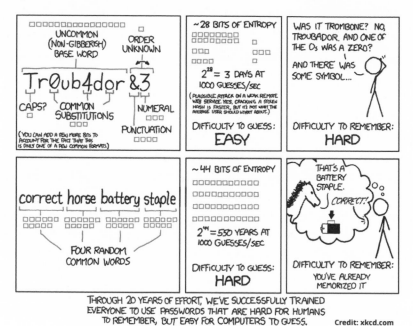

THROUGH 20 YEARS OF EFFORT, WE'VE SUCCESSFULLY TRAINED EVERYONE TO USE PASSWORDS THAT ARE HARD FOR HUMANS TO REMEMBER, BUT EASY FOR COMPUTERS TO GUESS.   Credit: xkcd.com

The things that we think of as hard are things that our brains aren't really wired to do, but we figured out ways to do anyway—things like math and physics and playing chess—but these things are trivially easy for a computer. It would be virtually impossible, for example, for a human to calculate π (pi) to a million decimal points, or memorize the geography of an entire city and calculate the fastest route from point A to point B, but a computer can do it in seconds.

On the other hand, the things that we think of as easy are things that our brains evolved for millions of years to be good at. This means that we have incredibly intricate and elaborate neural circuitry for doing them, so efficiently that the task seems trivial until we put it in front of a computer. For example, take the challenge of reading this word or telling which animal in the image below is a dog. Piece of cake for us, yet impossibly hard for a computer.

Gotcha captcha

What sorts of tasks are unlikely to be ceded to computers in the coming decades? In 1999, Dave Snowden, a Welsh management consultant, developed what has been called a "sense-making device" that draws on research in systems theory, complexity theory, network theory, and learning theories called the Cynefin framework. It divides the world into four decision-making contexts or "domains:"

1. **Obvious**, where there is a clear relationship between cause and effect, meaning that best practices can be easily documented, and solutions can be applied algorithmically.

2. **Complicated**, where analysis and investigation based on training and expertise are required to identify the relationship between cause and effect.

3. **Complex**, where the relationship between cause and effect are clear only in retrospect, and problems are solved by trialing new solutions.

4. **Chaotic**, where there is no clear relationship between cause and effect, but we have to act anyway.[63]

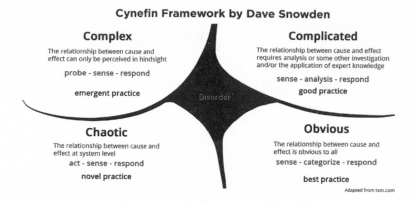

Cynefin Framework by Dave Snowden

Complex

The relationship between cause and effect can only be perceived in hindsight

probe - sense - respond

emergent practice

Disorder

Complicated

The relationship between cause and effect requires analysis or some other investigation and/or the application of expert knowledge

sense - analysis - respond

good practice

Chaotic

The relationship between cause and effect at system level

act - sense - respond

novel practice

Obvious

The relationship between cause and effect is obvious to all

sense - categorize - respond

best practice

Adapted from txm.com

Since the twentieth century, the working world has rotated through these domains. The first to fall to technology was the obvious tasks, and the rise in credentialism (i.e. degrees) originated with the need to train people for complicated work. Now intelligent machines and algorithms are starting to play in the realms of the complicated and sometimes even the complex, which is where massive job loss is going to come. In other words, it isn't jobs as a whole that are going away, so much as what Dutch historian Rutger Bregman, author of *Utopia for Realists*, calls "bullshit jobs" that dumb us down and drain us of our humanity.[64]

There will still be lots for us to do in the complex and chaotic domains that computers can't handle. But we need a very different set of skills in order to do them, and sadly today's education isn't doing a great job of empowering us with those skills. As British-American entrepreneur Andrew Keen writes in *How to Fix the Future*:

> The truth, however, in America at least, is that the children aren't being taught well. A May 2017 Pew Research Center report, *The Future of Jobs and Jobs Training*, asked 1,408 senior American executives, college professors, and AI experts a series of questions about the challenges of educating people for an automated world. The Pew report found that 30 percent of them expressed no confidence that schools, universities, and job training will evolve sufficiently quickly to match the demand for workers over the next decade. "Bosses believe your

work skills will soon be useless," the Washington Post bluntly concluded about the report.[65]

How should we approach this challenge? How do we go about preparing students for jobs that don't exist yet, using technologies that haven't been invented, in order to solve problems we don't even know are problems yet?

EDUCATION FOR THE PRESENT AND FUTURE

In 1971, political philosopher John Rawls proposed a thought experiment for designing a perfectly just society: Imagine that you know nothing about the particular talents, abilities, tastes, social class, and positions that you will be born with. Now design a political system. This exercise, called the "veil of ignorance," works because when you don't know which place in society you might end up, you'll take care to design a system that is fair, just, and compassionate to everyone.

It's a clever approach, so we'll take a page from Rawls' book to design the perfect education for the future. Imagine that you're about to undertake the most important project of your life and career. It is high-profile and sensitive, and it holds great potential for both upside and downside... and that's all you know about it. Nothing relating to the specific field of operation, scope of work, or tasks involved. Now select the people you would want to work on it as part of your team. Because you don't know anything about the specifics of the project, specialized skills aren't useful as selection criteria. It doesn't make sense to recruit a mechanical engineer when the project might have nothing to do with mechanical engineering. So other than basic foundational knowledge such as literacy and numeracy, you'll probably select for the softer skills, like creativity and resourcefulness, work ethic and reliability, learning and adaptability, and the ability to lead and play well with others. Or, put more eloquently by Andrew Keen:

> The challenge (and opportunity) for educators, then, is to teach everything that can't be replicated by a robot or an algorithm.

For Carr, with his vision of the profound limitations of computers, that includes the nurturing of intuition, ambiguity, and self-awareness. For Daniel Straub, the former Montessori educator, it is the teaching of consciousness and the idea of a calling. And for Union Square Ventures' Albert Wenger, who is homeschooling his three teenagers, it's teaching the self-mastery enabled by psychological freedom. This is the humanist ideal of education [Thomas] More laid out five hundred years ago in *Utopia*. It's the teaching of the unquantifiable: how to talk to one's peers, how to realize self-discipline, how to enjoy leisure, how to think independently, how to be a good citizen.[66]

This is precisely the sort of thought exercise that we need in order to "skate to where the puck is going."

You might think, "But how could I possibly build a team for a project without knowing anything about what it will entail?" Yet that's exactly what educators must do. When looking at a complex and chaotic future in which our students will solve problems that we don't yet know are problems with technologies that haven't been invented, this is precisely the sort of thought exercise that we need in order to "skate to where the puck is going."

NOT SO HYPOTHETICAL AFTER ALL

And it turns out that this hypothetical exercise isn't so hypothetical after all, because these are precisely the skills that lead to career success. Research conducted by Harvard University, the Carnegie Foundation, and Stanford Research Center has concluded that 85 percent of job success comes from having well-developed soft skills and people skills.[67] And eighteen months after being hired, 54 percent were discharged, and in 89 percent of cases it was because of attitude rather than skill.[68] As Ryan Craig reports:

> According to Peter Cappelli, director of the University of Pennsylvania Wharton School's Center for Human Resources and former co-director of the US Department of Education's

National Center on the Educational Quality of the Workforce:
[The employers'] list is topped not by a cluster of missing technical or academic abilities but by a lack of work attitude and
self-management skills such as punctuality, time management,
motivation and a strong work ethic. Indeed, the absence of
these traits, which used to be called 'character issues,' repeatedly shows up as a primary concern in numerous studies.[69]

That is probably why employers are so desperately searching for
candidates with these skills. In 2009 the Business Roundtable conducted a survey asking employers to rank the most important work
skills missing among recent high school graduates. The biggest com-
plaints were about attitudes and self-management skills. We have to
go down to the eighth item on the list to find something that might
be taught explicitly in schools (oral communication) and fourteenth
on the list to find a traditional academic subject (reading skills).[70]
In a 2013 study, 93 percent of employers agreed that candidates who
demonstrate a capacity to think critically, communicate clearly, and
solve complex problems are more important than their undergraduate
major.[71] And in an annual survey by Express Employment conducted
in April of 2017, employers were asked to rank twenty factors they
consider when making hiring decisions. Consistent with the results of
the past several years, work ethic was at the top of the list.[72] As Joseph
Aoun further explained:

> According to a 2016 survey of employers, the skill cited as most
> desirable in recent college graduates is the very human qual-
> ity of "leadership." More than 80 percent of respondents said
> they looked for evidence of leadership on candidates' résumés,
> followed by "ability to work in a team" at nearly 79 percent...
> Written communication and problem solving—skills more
> commonly attributed to a liberal arts education than a purely
> technical one—clocked in next at 70 percent. Curiously, tech-
> nical skills ranked in the middle of the survey, below strong
> work ethic or initiative.[73]

The verdict is clear: To succeed in the Age of Acceleration we need soft skills, and the intangible but critical things like work ethic and initiative. Employers know this, but there's just one little problem: The majority of the items on this list are generally considered to be traits that people either have or don't. This fundamental reorientation of *what* we want education to achieve has led to big changes in *how* that education is conceived and delivered. We'll explore those changes in the next chapter.

DID YOU GET ALL THAT? (LEARNING SELF-ASSESSMENT)

Want to test your understanding of the ideas that we just covered? Or start conversations with interested friends and colleagues? Here are a few questions to guide you:

1. Why is it so very hard to imagine what the distant future might look like?

2. Why is it important for educators to understand the implications of sensors, artificial intelligence, and automation on the global economy?

3. What are the technologies that are making driverless cars an imminent possibility?

4. Thomas Friedman describes four directions in which jobs are being pulled by various technologies. What are these directions?

5. A 2013 Oxford University whitepaper forecasts that 47 percent of jobs could be eliminated by technology in the next two decades. What kinds of jobs are likely to be technology-proof?

6. What is the Budding Effect?

7. What sort of things are hard for us, but trivially easy for a computer?

8. What sort of things are trivial for humans to do, but very hard for computers?

9. Describe the four domains of decision-making according to the Cynefin framework.

10. Of the four domains under Cynefin framework, which ones are going to be difficult for computers to handle? Why?

11. What is the Veil of Ignorance, and what does it have to do with the future of education?

12. Why are soft skills more likely than technical skills to be valuable in the workplace of the future?

13. Based on surveys, what skills and qualities do employers find most important?

LIKE WHAT YOU READ, AND WANT TO GO DEEPER?

Here are a few good books to take a look at if you'd like to go deeper on some of the ideas presented in this chapter.

1. Thomas Friedman's *Thank You For Being Late*

2. Joseph E. Aoun's *Robot-Proof*

3. Martin Ford's *Rise of the Robots*

4. Klaus Schwab's *The Fourth Industrial Revolution*

For more information, including this entire book in digital format plus actionable conversation video guides at the end of each chapter, an expanded and up-to-date bibliography, and additional resources, visit LeveragedLearningBook.com

The Changing Landscape of Learning

"btw, forgot to tell u... click ur heels together 3 times and u can go home" –Glinda

"Mom, where are you??? I woke up and nobody's here!" –Kevin

"Sorry hun, had to run–midnite curfew. Call me tmrw? also I think I lost my shoe." –Cinderella

"Harry, it was just a dream. I'm fine. Don't storm the Ministry." –Sirius Black

"Hey Alfred, Bruce got scared by the opera, can you come pick us up in front?" –Thomas Wayne

"Romeo, I came up with a plan with Friar Laurence. I'm not really dead–lol. Just fyi." –Juliet

FEW THINGS have been as disruptive to story plots as the instant information sharing made possible by text messaging. Just a single text, and Dorothy would never have met the Scarecrow, the Tin Man, or the Cowardly Lion. Kevin's parents would have known that he was okay, and no murdered parents would have meant no traumatized Bruce Wayne, and therefore no Batman.

Of course, stories might get away with it from time to time, coming up with weird twists explaining why none of the characters have cellular service, or even a phone. But it's the sort of narrative device that strains credibility and must be used sparingly. We all know that the world today isn't the same as it was a few decades ago, so we must adapt. The same is true of the way we conceive and consume education.

There are four major transitions currently changing the landscape of learning, with the same seismic implications to education as the instant information sharing of text messaging to plots of movies. Each of these transitions underscores shifts in what we want and expect as consumers of education, challenges for institutions who provide it, and opportunities for upstarts to enter the scene.

TRANSITION #1: FROM REAL-TIME TO SEMI-SYNCHRONOUS

Have you ever noticed how quickly most restaurants can get any number of dishes ready? Sure, some of this is customer service sleight-of-hand, starting you off with bread or nachos or salad to distract you from waiting for your meal. Even taking that into account, and considering the rush time or occasionally incompetent waiter, it's rare for a restaurant to need more than ten to twenty minutes to prepare any given dish.

It's so common that we take it for granted, but the next time you're in a restaurant, take a moment to consider the items on the menu and ask yourself, assuming you had the recipe and all the ingredients, how long it would take to prepare the same dish at home. With rare exceptions, the answer is much, much longer. So how do restaurants get the job done so quickly?

The answer is in the *mise en place*, a French culinary term that translates to "everything in its place." Take a relatively simple dish like an Italian spaghetti primavera, for example. The pasta just needs to be dropped in boiling water for a few minutes. The sauce, however, is more complex. You might start by sautéing onions in oil and garlic, then adding carrots, zucchini, mushrooms, broccoli, and more. A fair amount of preparation is required before you can start cooking: taking the ingredients out of the refrigerator and cupboard, peeling and crushing the garlic, and chopping all the vegetables. That part usually adds up to more time and work than the actual cooking of the meal!

Restaurants know this, so they get things done in advance. The chef doesn't receive your order for spaghetti primavera and start taking ingredients out of the fridge. The *mise en place* has already been prepared and placed in little dishes by junior kitchen staffers, ready to go.

This process is effective because it neatly divides the work of food preparation into two categories: the tasks that need to happen in *real-time* (the actual cooking that leads to a fresh, hot meal) and the tasks that can be done *semi-synchronously*, meaning within the bounds of a much wider window (laying out and preparing all the ingredients). Now, it usually isn't a good idea to do everything a-synchronously (think of how unappetizing microwave dinners often are). But as recent meal-kit providers like HelloFresh and Blue Apron are capitalizing upon, there are compelling time and efficiency savings to be achieved by a-synchronously doing the things that easily can be. The process is the same reason that we generally prefer YouTube and DVRs and Netflix over live television, text messages and email over phone conversations, and Uber over the bus. It works for food, entertainment, communication, and transportation as well as for education.

SEMI-SYNCHRONOUS: A NEW SPIN ON AN OLD IDEA

The idea of non-synchronous education has been around since at least 1844, when Sir Isaac Pitman founded his Correspondence Colleges in England.[74] However, a certificate from Pitman's Correspondence Colleges back then didn't carry any more weight than most online courses did as recently as five or ten years ago; it was too far outside the mainstream. Distance learning finally has started to change, thanks to the efforts of MOOCs like Coursera and edX, course platforms such as MasterClass, Udemy and LinkedIn Learning (formerly Lynda.com), and myriad boutique course providers on a plethora of topics, including my own company, Mirasee, in the area of business education. A good parallel for the mainstream acceptance of online courses today is the state of online dating a few years ago; past the point of being odd or taboo, but not yet something that everybody did, and definitely not responsible for nearly one in five marriages.[75]

This widespread acceptance is partly a matter of familiarity and partly a matter of convenience, but also largely a reflection of the fact that many features of online courses are just plain better. As Bryan Caplan writes, "Online education has clear pedagogical advantages over traditional education"[76]—advantages like the ability to cost-effectively run "flipped classrooms." Students consume the lesson content on their own time, using video that they can pause, rewind, accelerate, and re-watch until they know they've got it, then engage with an instructor or their peers. It's not just any old instructor: Now we can engage the best instructors in the world and make their course materials accessible to as many people as want to participate, regardless of their location, time zone, or schedule.

> Now we can engage the best instructors in the world and make their course materials accessible to as many people as want to participate.

We've been in the 1.0 days of online education, and there's still an enormous amount of room for growth and improvement. At the top of the list is that line between a-synchronous and semi-synchronous.

You can prepare the *mise en place* for your spaghetti primavera within a much wider window than the moments before you begin to cook, but that doesn't mean you can do it anytime. Ingredients can lose their freshness and go bad, so while you can prepare them that day, and maybe earlier that week, it would be a mistake to take a completely a-synchronous approach and chop vegetables for an entire year. Similarly, while much of education can be done semi-synchronously, some things still work best in real-time and face to face. The blending of the two options creates the perfect balance of convenience, affordability, and effectiveness.

Semi-synchronous education also leads to the second major transition in the learning landscape, from just-in-case to just-in-time.

TRANSITION #2: FROM JUST-IN-CASE TO JUST-IN-TIME

In 1972, Maureen and Tony Wheeler bought a beat-up car and drove from London "as far east as we could go."[77] They wound up in Australia, and along the way they jotted notes about the best things to see, places to eat, and activities to participate in. The couple loved adventure and wanted to discover the world for themselves. Not everyone wants quite that level of adventure, though, and the Wheelers' notes formed the foundations of an attractive guidebook for people who wanted to discover the world without figuring it all out on their own. That was the beginning of Lonely Planet, the travel guide company.

When it comes to travel, I'm on the opposite end of the spectrum in my appetite for novelty and adventure. The idea of being dropped into an unfamiliar environment and figuring it all out on the fly can bring me close to a panic attack. Most of my travel is for business, and I want to get from the airport to my hotel, with as little adventure along the way as possible.

Thankfully, the combination of credit cards, Google Maps, Booking.com, Uber, extensive cellular connectivity, and the ability to search for any information you might need when you need it have made travel almost as smooth an experience as someone of my temperament can hope for. Let's say I was invited to attend a conference for my first visit to Australia, for example. I wouldn't need to do much other than pack a bag, get on a plane, and figure the rest out upon arrival. That's the beauty of our age of *just-in-time* information and services: Pre-planning is often unnecessary and overrated.

There are a couple of notable exceptions, though. As a Canadian, it would be important for me to know before my trip that I need to arrange a visa to enter the country, that Australia's location in the Southern Hemisphere means the seasons are flipped (Canada's winter is Australia's summer, and vice versa), and that unlike the spiders occasionally encountered in my hometown of Montreal, many spiders in Australia are venomous and should be avoided. Just-in-time is too late for these things; they're important to know *just-in-case*. Otherwise I might be turned away at the airport, pack for the wrong weather, or suffer an unpleasant bite.

This is the second major transition in the world of education: from just-in-case to just-in-time. Learning used to be something that you did for a long time at the start of your career, but that just doesn't work in today's world. It's so much easier to access information and training when we need it, and conditions change so quickly that things you learned "just-in-case" are more likely than not to be outdated and irrelevant by the time you actually need them. This isn't a fringe idea, but rather one espoused even in the academic establishment; Lawrence Summers, former president of Harvard University, went on record saying, "I think, increasingly, anything you learn is going to become obsolete within a decade, and so the most important kind of learning is how to learn."[78] As Jeff Cobb, author of *Leading the Learning Revolution* explains:

> For decades we've lived in a 'knowledge economy,' one driven by service and information-based businesses. But now knowledge sounds too finite, there are professions where knowledge

Anything you learn is going to become obsolete within a decade.

still works, but we now live in a 'figure it out on a daily basis' economy, or a learning economy. The nature of our work is changing from year to year, based off the development of technology.[79]

And it gets worse – not only is much of what we learn "just-in-case" as likely as not to be outdated by the time we need it, but also, as Rohit Bhargava elaborates in *Always Eat Left Handed*, the odds that we'll need much of it are almost as slim as the odds that we'll remember it if we do:

> Since early in grade school, our education is very infrequently connected directly to the world around us. Much of this education is "just-in-case"—things that we learn either because of tradition or the mistaken belief that that one day we may need to know them or choose a profession that uses them. Calculus, the history of Mesopotamia, how to spot iambic pentameter … these are all pieces of knowledge that you may or may not use through the course of your life. Sadly, if a moment arises in the future where you did need to know about any of those topics, chances are you wouldn't remember enough of what you learned years ago in order for it to be useful anyway.[80]

THE TRANSITION TO LIFELONG LEARNING

So if not a mass of education at the start of our careers, then what? As Joseph Aoun, president of Northeastern University in Boston, writes, "It no longer is sufficient for universities to focus solely on isolated years of study for undergraduate and graduate students."[81] The answer is education in smaller increments, spread over our entire lives—what Jeff Cobb calls the "other 50 years."[82] This probably will add up to more education in aggregate; the Stanford 2025 project of reimagining the future of education, for example, predicts that the current four years during the ages from 18 to 22 will be replaced by six years spread over a lifetime.[83]

This transition to lifelong just-in-time education is underway, as we see from the percentage of increasingly older students partaking in education. Currently 17 percent of the $1.4 trillion of outstanding student loan debt in the United States belongs to people older than 50, and people older than 60 are the fastest-growing age segment of the student loan market.[84] As Aoun writes:

> Of the 20.5 million students attending U.S. colleges and universities in 2016, 8.2 million were 25 years or older. A full 40 percent of students, therefore, are older than the age generally viewed as 'traditional' for college. By 2025, the number of students aged 25 or older is projected to increase to 9.7 million.[85]

But in a context of lifelong learning, taking a full-time semester for skill development is impractical, to say nothing of one or more years. So courses are shortened and designed to be done on the side, while the rest of life continues to go on. This is the granularization of learning, what Bhargava calls "light-speed learning." In his words, "The road to mastery on any topic gets faster through the help of bite-sized learning modules that make education more time efficient, engaging, useful and fun."[86] Familiar examples are the courses on platforms like Udemy and Lynda, or those provided by independent professionals. And on the far extreme of granularity is the rising interest in microlearning and learning through apps, like DuoLingo and Smart.ly.

THE NEW EDUCATION ECOSYSTEM

So if the consumption of education is trending away from four years at the start of one's career to something in the range of six years over the course of a lifetime… how will those six years be distributed to have impact and meaning in the students' lives? Most likely, education will divide into three categories: foundational, "last mile," and continuing:

Foundational education is the stuff that everybody needs: fundamental knowledge and skills, the ability to generate insight from whatever else you might learn, and the fortitude that is at the core of surviving and thriving in the world. This is what universities today say they do and even try to do, but fail miserably, in terms of both absolute results and return on the time and money invested.

"Last mile" education (hat tip to Ryan Craig, who coined the term[87]) is the technical training that bridges the gap between a well-rounded foundation and the specific skills that are needed to enter specific career paths. This is currently offered in clunky fashion by law schools and medical schools, as well as by coding boot camps and apprenticeship programs. They may not be efficient or pretty, but these are the bridges from a general education into a specific career.

Continuing education is what we all need in order to stay current in a world where "anything you learn is going to become obsolete within a decade."[88] Currently, this is a mess of executive education, learning on the job, self-study from books and YouTube videos, personal practice, certifications from a smattering of sources, and a variety of online courses from a range of providers, with little in the way of oversight or quality control.

Foundational ➡ "Last Mile" ➡ Continuing

There's much to be done in all these areas to get to where we need to be. However, we can expect that in the not-too-distant future, a lifelong educational path will begin with one or two years of foundational and "last mile" education, either taken separately or bundled together, with four more years spread over the rest of our lives and careers.

TRANSITION #3: FROM INFORMATION TO TRANSFORMATION

Ashlee "Tree" Branch graduated *summa cum laude* with a grade point average of 3.941 from High Point University in North Carolina. She had worked hard at her studies, and also worked during her studies as an assistant in the school's Office of Student Life, then in the Women's and Gender Studies Department. So her resume was as strong as you can expect a fresh graduate to be when she set out into the workforce in search of a career. She quickly encountered the frustrating Catch-22 facing almost every young job seeker: Employers don't want to hire you unless you have experience, but of course you can't get experience until someone takes the chance to hire you. The story ended well for Tree, and for me; she's a superstar, and when her resume came across my desk in October of 2015, I had the good sense to hire her, and we haven't looked back since.

The Catch-22 is challenging and real. Yes, recent graduates have lots of things working against them: the enormous average student debt, the ubiquity of degrees making it hard for them to stand out, and the general misalignment of college curricula with the skills that employers are actually looking for. But employers have an even bigger and more fundamental issue with people fresh out of school: They just don't know anything. Or rather, they know a whole lot, but they don't know how to *do* anything. To quote Stephen R. Covey, "To know and not to do is really not to know."

The value of information alone has cratered. In fairness, knowledge used to be a lot more valuable than it is today. Back when my *World Book Encyclopedia* was the best way to find information that I needed, it made perfect sense to pay a premium for the 26-volume set. But those days are long gone. Today we have Google and Wikipedia, with anything we might want to know is just a few keystrokes or a voice command away, the value of information alone has cratered. What really matters is our ability to do something with what we know, and that's a different kettle of fish.

LEARNING ABOUT VS. LEARNING TO

Pure knowledge is fairly easy to impart. All it takes is a good explanation and possibly a bit of repetition, and you've got it. Everything you've read in this book so far is a good example of this. I hope that my explanations have been clear, engaging, and cogent enough for you to feel that you're getting a grasp on what's wrong with education today, and how it is changing. But that doesn't mean you're capable yet of doing something about it. For that you'll need a lot more than just an explanation!

Developing a competence or skill can start with an explanation and repetition, but it also needs the input and experience of real-world application, a feedback loop that tells whether you're on the right track or need to correct your course, and gives you the opportunity to make those adjustments and see the results. Although most of the world of education does a decent job of imparting knowledge, it isn't very good at imparting skill.

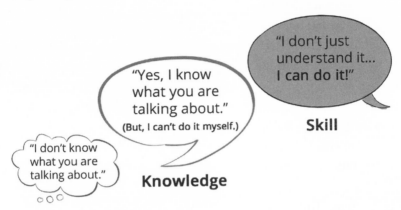

For that sort of learning, a classroom doesn't cut it. Rather, we need experiential education. While representing a minority of the overall education that's out there today, experiential education is most commonly done through some variation of an apprenticeship or internship, whether it's cooperative education, part-time or short-term internships, job shadowing, study-abroad programs, service and service learning, or undergraduate research projects.[89] When they're done well, they can be hugely influential and valuable, but most of the time, they aren't done well at all.

At worst, they're a way for companies to get cheap labor, schools to benefit from a bit of arbitrage, and students to waste a whole bunch of time filing, fetching coffee, or otherwise doing tasks that have little to do with the skills and expertise that they're supposed to learn.

Of course, some internships are a lot better; they involve students in interesting and relevant work, and give them the opportunity to gain hands-on, real-life experience. This is extremely valuable for the students, but still a cop-out for the teachers, who basically are conceding that they can't design a curriculum more effective than just dropping the student into a real-life situation and hoping for the best. That is fine, but it obviates the need for the instructor!

Only the best of these programs alternate real-world experience with relevant classroom learning and deconstruction of that experience (sometimes called a "blended learning" model), which is what it really takes for this model to work well. And we need it to work, because if students don't experience a real transformation, there's no point to the education. Which is especially tough, because transformation for one person might not be transformation for another.

THE JAGGED PATH TO TRANSFORMATION

In 2006, Sir Ken Robinson stepped onto the red dot that marks center stage at the TED conference, to deliver his now famous talk titled *Do schools kill creativity?* He recounted the story of Gillian Lynne. As a child in the 1930s, Gillian couldn't stop fidgeting. The school complained to Gillian's mother, who took her to see a specialist. After a lengthy conversation with Gillian's mother, the specialist left Gillian alone in a room, and turned on the radio. He and Gillian's mother watched as she started dancing to the music, leading to his diagnosis: "She isn't sick," he told Mrs. Lynne, "she's a dancer."

That diagnosis turned out to be right on the money. Gillian Lynne grew up to become one of the most successful choreographers in history, with major broadway credits to her name like *Cats* and *Phantom of the Opera*. The learning specialist in this story should be commended, for two reasons. The first is that he didn't diagnose her as sick and put her on whatever the 1930s equivalent of Ritalin would have been. The second, though, is that he had the insight to see a special talent that was unique to Gillian.

In the previous chapter explored how being relevant in the modern age requires that we lean into the things that we're good at, and computers aren't. But we aren't all good at the same things. This is the research focus of Harvard professor Todd Rose. Whereas most learning experiences are designed around the idea that people are more or less the same, Rose argues that no one is truly average—we're all strong in some areas, and weak in others.[90] One person might have exceptional reading and writing abilities, yet be frustrated by the spatial reasoning required in geometry. Another student might love science and dream of running her own experiments, while also being a slow reader who gets flummoxed by the explanations in textbooks. Yet another person might have trouble sitting still in class, but have the potential to be one of the world's greatest choreographers.

For learning to be truly transformative, then, it has to be customized around the unique strengths and opportunities available to the learner in question. Which has the added benefit of being more engaging to the student, at a time when just holding a student's attention is getting harder and harder.

TRANSITION #4: FROM MANDATORY TO VOLITIONAL

In 2011, Sebastian Thrun's *Introduction to Artificial Intelligence* course at Stanford University was made freely available online to anyone who wanted to participate. The 160,000 registrants were enough of an impetus for Thrun to leave Stanford and found a massive open online course (MOOC) company called Udacity. His work was so impressive and inspiring that the following year he won the Smithsonian American Ingenuity Award in Education.[91]

By 2013 the bloom was coming off the rose. Despite having signed up 1.6 million students for his online classes, he decided to pivot away from MOOCs. Why? Quite simply, the concept didn't seem to work; only seven percent of students in the online courses actually made it to the end.[92] Udacity wasn't unique in this regard; a fair amount of investigation has shown that the completion rate of MOOCs across the board tends to max out at 15 percent.[93] To put that in perspective, even the abysmal graduation rates of for-profit colleges such as the University of Phoenix see an online course completion rate of 17 percent.[94] The model of a massively open online course seemed flawed, so Thrun turned his attention to new opportunities like nanodegrees.

Why are MOOC completion rates so incredibly low? Do students not want to learn? Are people fundamentally incapable of following through on ventures that they set out to do? Maybe the reason is a lot simpler: perhaps MOOCs just offer too much freedom and choice.

Consider this: For almost the entire history of education, it wasn't optional. Take K-12 education, for example. Laws vary from jurisdiction to jurisdiction, but by and large parents are considered criminally negligent if their children don't go to school. So as kids, we go because we must. The same is true of continuing education provided by employers; if your boss tells you to go, and you want to keep your job, you go. No questions asked.

Then there's the education that isn't quite mandatory, but almost. For example, attending college isn't a legal requirement, but it is so ingrained into the culture that many people feel as if it needs to be done, no matter the cost. There's also the matter of sunk cost, and how much of an investment we can afford to abandon. Even if undergraduate or graduate education isn't technically mandatory, once we've signed the papers and taken on the debt, we're committed.

But as we saw in the transition from just-in-case to just-in-time, education is changing from a single decision to participate in a four-year program at the start of a career, to a combined total of six years worth of education in in small increments, comprised of and dozens of individual decisions across our lifetimes.[95] Rather than the commitment that comes from tens of thousands of dollars of debt plus tens of thousands of dollars of opportunity cost, each decision comes at a cost of hundreds or thousands of dollars plus a few weeks or months of part-time commitment. It's not that we set out to lose time or money, but these are amounts that we can afford to walk away from.

We used to have structure imposed on us as well; once you start a class, you know that you must be in Room 407 every Tuesday at 3 p.m.

But as courses go online and semi-synchronous, as with MOOCs, you can start anytime, consume the lessons whenever you want, and take as long as you like to go through the entire the course. The choice and freedom to dictate everything about our educational journey is great for creating accessibility, but challenging in imposing the burden of self-management on students who aren't ready for it.

NO, ATTENTION SPANS AREN'T SHRINKING

> Our so-called "shrinking attention spans" aren't a measure of distractibility, but rather of discernment.

Perhaps you've heard the Internet statistic that our attention spans are shorter than that of a goldfish. This is total nonsense, and anyone who believes we have dwindling attention spans in an age of binge-watching hours of shows on Netflix needs to re-evaluate personal assumptions. The statistic comes from the sensationalization and misreading of a 2015 study conducted by Microsoft, which showed that it took about eight and a half seconds for the subjects' attention to wander from whatever was put in front of them.[96] Our so-called "shrinking attention spans" aren't a measure of distractibility, but rather of discernment. What it really tells us is that it took eight and a half seconds for the participants' minds to begin wondering if there might be something more interesting or worthy of their attention.

That's a challenging reality for many educational experiences, which have had the luxury of a captive audience that made it unreasonably easy to compete for their students' attention because they didn't have to. But now they do because the competition to a lecture, training, or video isn't the instructor down the hall. Every time we log into a class takes willpower, and how our experience with each lesson, positive or negative, measures up against the alternatives of catching up on Netflix, viewing TED Talks videos, or playing games affects how much willpower we'll need to log in the next time.

There are two approaches that course creators can take to overcome this challenge. The first is to take away some choice, by bringing back start dates, end dates, and deadlines that must be met to remain a student in good standing. In other words, it's dialing back from a-synchronous to semi-synchronous. This is a key factor why Seth Godin's altMBA boasts completion rates of 96 percent.[97]

The second approach is to develop courses engaging enough for students to choose them over everything else vying for their attention. This is difficult and expensive, requiring a combination of excellent and/or celebrity instructors, planning and storyboarding, interaction and community. Good early examples of work being done in this area can be found with MasterClass and with Jumpcut, a Los Angeles-based startup.

The way that education is being delivered is shifting from real-time to semi-synchronous, from just-in-case to just-in-time, from information to transformation, and from mandatory to volitional. That's a lot of changes, and each is as disruptive to the educational status quo as a phone with text messaging capabilities would have been to the plots of *The Wizard of Oz*, *Home Alone*, or *Batman*. None of these are hypothetical cases or futuristic guesses. They're all here now, changing the process of how we consume and deliver education.

In the last chapter we explored the changes to *what* we teach, and now we've also covered the changes to *how* we teach. There's one very important question to answer, which is: *who* will provide the education of the future? The next two chapters will answer that question, through an exploration of the economics of education.

The Four Transitions in Education

Real-Time	➡	Semi-Synchronous
Just-in-Case	➡	Just-in-Time
Information	➡	Transformation
Mandatory	➡	Volitional

DID YOU GET ALL THAT? (LEARNING SELF-ASSESSMENT)

Want to test your understanding of the ideas that we just covered? Or start conversations with interested friends and colleagues? Here are a few questions to guide you:

1. What are the four transitions that are reshaping the landscape of learning?

2. What are the pedagogical advantages of online education over traditional education?

3. How is semi-synchronous different from real-time or a-synchronous education?

4. What is the difference between just-in-case and just-in-time education?

5. People used to prepare for careers by undertaking four years of focused studies during the ages of 18-22. According to the Stanford 2025 project on the future of education, what will this be replaced with?

6. Why is information ("learning about") no longer enough as an outcome of education?

7. What is meant by "experiential" education?

8. The typical completion rates of online courses are dismal, usually ranging from 7-15 percent. Why is that?

9. "Humans have shorter attention spans than a goldfish." True or False? Why?

10. What are the two approaches online course creators can take to improve completion rates?

LIKE WHAT YOU READ, AND WANT TO GO DEEPER?

Here are a few good books to take a look at if you'd like to go deeper on some of the ideas presented in this chapter.

- Jeff Cobb's *Leading the Learning Revolution*

- James Stellar's *Education That Works*

For more information, including this entire book in digital format plus actionable conversation video guides at the end of each chapter, an expanded and up-to-date bibliography, and additional resources, visit LeveragedLearningBook.com.

CHAPTER 4

Economics of the New Education

THE EARLY American automotive industry was largely shaped by two men: Henry Ford and William C. Durant. Neither invented the automobile, but between them, they built the foundations of an industry that has endured for more than a hundred years.

Henry Ford's story is well known. His Ford Motor Company was incorporated in 1903, joining the hundreds of companies seeking to capitalize on the automobile opportunity. On October 1, 1908, the first Ford Model T was completed at the company's Piquette Avenue plant in Detroit. It was a good car for its time, but the real innovation came next: By 1913, the car transitioned to mass production on a moving assembly line. By 1927, more than fifteen million Model T automobiles had been produced—the longest production run of any car model in history until the Volkswagen Beetle in 1972.

Ford's resume prior to founding his company is conspicuously lacking in experience with the horse-drawn carriage, which was the mainstream transportation industry of the time. He grew up on his family's farm in Michigan, but he hated farm work and left home. He was always mechanically inclined. At the age of fifteen he dismantled and reassembled the clocks and watches of friends and neighbors, gaining the reputation of a watch repairman. He worked in a series of mechanical jobs, and at twenty-eight he was hired as an engineer by the Edison Illuminating Company, where he tinkered with a self-propelled vehicle that he called the Ford Quadricycle. Five years later, he was introduced to Thomas Edison, who approved of his automobile experimentation, which eventually led Ford to strike out on his own.

Then there's William C. Durant. Together with J. Dallas Dort, he founded the Durant-Dort Carriage Company in 1886. By 1900, it was the largest manufacturer in the industry, producing as many as 56,000 horse-drawn carriages per year. But that didn't last long; seventeen years later they manufactured their last carriage. Automobiles were filling the streets, and the horse-drawn carriage industry was dying.

That wasn't the end of Durant's story. Possessing a keen eye for opportunity, he came to own several Ford dealerships between 1903 and 1908. Seeing the writing on the wall, and wealthy from his carriage company success, he capitalized General Motors as a holding company on September 16, 1908. The next day GM acquired the Buick Motor Company, and it rapidly acquired more than twenty companies, including Oldsmobile, Cadillac, and Oakland, which later was named Pontiac. Durant was forced out of the company in 1911, so he partnered with Louis Chevrolet to start the Chevrolet Motor Company in 1915 and returned to GM the following year.

The contrast between these two founders of the automotive industry reflects an important question: Where does innovation usually come from? Is it from inside an industry, like Durant, or from elsewhere, like Ford? In other words, who was the exception, and who was the rule?

HISTORY IS FULL OF FORDS, NOT DURANTS

In the world of politics, incumbents—those who already hold office and are seeking re-election—have significant advantages over challengers. Part of it is their name recognition and reputation, part is their ability to reach far more people with their message, and part is the financial resources that their incumbency affords. In aggregate, the effect is that since the 1960s, at least 80 percent of incumbents have defeated their challengers in every American congressional election.[98]

The advantages of incumbency generalize beyond the world of politics in two ways: reach and resources. Incumbents, like Durant in the transportation industry in the early 1900s, have established reputation, relationships, and infrastructure that allow them to reach more customers, and their past success affords them substantial financial and other resources to lean on. While Ford had to build his company more or less from scratch, Durant had the resources to buy Buick, Oldsmobile, and Cadillac and consolidate them into General Motors. These are all reasons why challengers might hesitate before getting in the ring with an eight hundred-pound incumbent.

Yet, in spite of those advantages, history is laden with examples of the incumbent being defeated by the innovator. Amazon came from outside of book publishing, iTunes came from outside of the music industry, and Uber challenged established taxi companies—and all met with incredible resistance. Airbnb wasn't created by the hotel industry, nor were TurboTax or LegalZoom created by big accounting or law firms. The computer mouse and graphical user interface were developed by Xerox, but their commercial success came with Apple and Microsoft. Similarly, digital photography technology was pioneered inside Kodak, but the company didn't do anything with it. And even though Blockbuster had the inventory and storage in place, it was Netflix that came out of nowhere with mail-order DVD rentals.

The list goes on, and on, and on, coming full circle to the automotive industry: While it started with an exciting bang, the last successful start-up car manufacturer was a little company in Detroit called Chrysler, founded in 1925. Almost exactly a century after the Ford Motor Company was founded, disruption came to an industry in desperate need in the form of a start-up in Palo Alto called Tesla. At its head was Elon Musk, a disruptive innovator and industry outsider in the tradition of Henry Ford.

The conclusion is clear: Durant was the exception, and Ford was the rule, despite the substantial advantages of incumbents. Which raises the question: In spite of all their advantages, why do incumbents often lose? A big factor is that right up to the end, it looks as though they're winning.

LEGACY, INERTIA, AND THE INNOVATOR'S DILEMMA

Imagine you're the despotic leader of a small, developing nation. From your subjects' perspective, the regime may be suboptimal, but from where you're sitting, things look pretty good. You have money, power, and almost anything else that you might wish for, except, of course, for the respect of your people. Although they may not like it, you have the advantages of an incumbent, which in your case includes tax collectors and soldiers. History has shown that periodic uprisings and protests can be handled with the iron fist of jailings and executions. So while the international community wags its finger, you shrug and continue business as usual.

With many challenges over time, the incumbent almost always falls.

In this situation, you're what Nassim Nicholas Taleb describes in *The Black Swan* as a "turkey." For a thousand days, the turkey is fed and fattened by the farmer. Life seems good for the turkey, who doesn't realize that every day brings it closer to slaughter. As Taleb writes, "Consider that [the turkey's] feeling of safety reached its maximum when the risk was highest!"[99] The same is true for the despot, who successfully quells any opposition right up to the moment when his head winds up on a pike!

Incumbents are like those despots and turkeys, seeing mounting validation that they're doing well until the rug gets pulled out from under them. In any particular encounter, like an individual political race, the strong advantage goes to the incumbent. But with many challenges over time, the incumbent almost always falls. Why are incumbents so blind and resistant to change that in the grand scheme of things is almost inevitable?

For starters, incumbents are generally invested in how things are currently done, and they stand to lose a lot when things change. From Blockbuster's perspective, quantifying the opportunity of mail-order DVD rentals is a lot harder and more speculative than the real risk of cannibalizing revenues from in-store rentals. Likewise, the loyalty benefit gained by eliminating late fees would be hard to enumerate, compared with the certainty down to the last cent in the dollars that would be lost by doing so. Compounding that, incumbents have substantial structures in place for doing things the old way. Doing things differently takes different systems and different skills, which means that the greater the incumbent's perceived advantages, the more costly the disruption (i.e. money and jobs) tends to be when changing direction toward a new model. This flies in the face of basic human self-interest. As Pulitzer-winning author Upton Sinclair said, "It is difficult to get a man to understand something, when his salary depends upon his not understanding it!"

There's also the challenge of opportunity blindness. A sense of "this is how we've always done things" quickly morphs into "and if there was a better way, we'd be doing it already." This creates a skepticism about new opportunities that seems backed by a track record of solid data, like the experiences of Taleb's turkey. Getting buy-in to change is difficult, and even if you can get it, it's hard to focus on multiple things at the same time, hence Clayton Christensen's recommendation in *The Innovator's Dilemma* that innovation in large organizations is best led in a secret, independent "skunkworks" division, which introduces its own set of challenges.

All these factors repeatedly have prevented innovation from coming to organizations that have every advantage—think Microsoft and the Internet, or Nokia and the iPhone—and we have every reason to believe that the same will be true in the realm of education.

Consider the structure that education will likely fall into, of a year or two of foundational and "last mile" education at the start of a career, followed by four years of continuing education, spread over the balance of a lifetime:

Foundational ➡ "Last Mile" ➡ Continuing

There's much to be done in all these areas to get to where we need to be. However, we can expect that in the not-too-distant future, a lifelong educational path will begin with one or two years of foundational and "last mile" education, either taken separately or bundled together, with four more years spread over the rest of our lives and careers. Who will provide these critical building blocks of education?

WHY COLLEGES AREN'T LIKELY TO INNOVATE

The most likely casualty of this shift in education are colleges and universities. With more than 40 percent of the global $4.4 trillion education market,[100] the higher education structure is an eight thousand-pound incumbent. As such, it is saddled with all the anchors and blinders that usually hamper incumbents from innovating, along with a few that are unique to this industry. There will be some exceptions who buck the trend—the William Durants in a world of Henry Fords. But most institutions of higher education today are like Nokia and Blackberry two years after the iPhone was introduced—still alive, but not heading anywhere good. They have too many things working against them for us to expect much in the way of innovation, including:

Cognitive inertia. The biggest strike against higher education is its legacy of success, and the blindness that creates to the need for change. Mid-career administrators and educators in the institutional system today grew up in the 1980s and 1990s, when the prospects and value of higher education were very different from what they are now. The deep feeling of something being the way it is can be hard to shake, and even mounting evidence can be rationalized away. Sure, there are 2.4 million fewer students enrolled in the American system than there were five years ago,[101] but there are still twenty million students in the system, which translates to about $600 billion per year. That's a pretty big number! And the precipitous decline in faculties like law may be an anomaly as a bellwether of things to come.

Research focus. There have been great historical reasons and great value in the fact that universities do double duty as both teaching and research institutions. However, the dual focus leads to a misalignment of incentives, which makes the innovation that is needed today exceptionally hard. Put simply, academics thrive when they research and publish, not when they teach. As Ryan Craig writes, this means that "while teaching undergraduates is normally a very large part of a professor's job, success in our field is correlated with a professor's ability to avoid teaching undergraduates."[102]

> "While teaching undergraduates is normally a very large part of a professor's job, success in our field is correlated with a professor's ability to avoid teaching undergraduates."

Lack of employability focus. The flip side to higher education's focus on research is the lack of focus on employability. Much as top-tier colleges like to tout the self-reported employment rates and salaries of their graduates, the reality is that caring about employability is primarily relegated to the university's marketing department and career services program, neither of which is anywhere close to the core of the institution's promise or experience.

Access to expertise. Even if colleges can overcome the cognitive inertia and want to change, most find themselves lacking the expertise to do so. The transition from just-in-case to just-in-time means that the only people with the expertise that students really need are the ones on the cutting edge of their industries. Generally speaking, those people are gainfully employed at places other than universities. If they moved to full-time teaching positions, it would take only a few years for their expertise to start going out of date.

Tenure. Let's say that institutions can overcome cognitive inertia, can find qualified experts who want to teach, and somehow can stay on the cutting edge of their field. Institutions are still constrained by the laws of tenure. The promise of a permanent position originally was designed to protect academic freedom, under the idea that it is beneficial for society if scholars are free to hold and examine a variety of views regardless of how they align with the orthodoxy of the day. That may be, but it also means that tenured professors can be terminated only for cause or under extraordinary circumstances. That translates to fewer job openings, and the tenured professors have great freedom to teach whatever aligns with their personal interests, as opposed to what students want and need to learn.

Accreditation. Accreditation is the original formalization of signal. As institutions of higher learning popped up across the country and around the world, the need arose for a way of validating which were the real deal. This led to the accreditation industry, which includes multiple examiners with different levels of prestige and accrediting bodies to supervise them.[103] Fundamentally, the way it works is that after a course is designed, the outline is shown to the accrediting bodies, who give it their stamp of approval. From that point on, the course content can be changed only so much without need to submit it for reaccreditation, which is adds another layer of bureaucracy to an overburdened process.

Massive cost burden. Finally, the incumbents evolved in a time when people looked for different things in their institutions of higher learning. Because the signal guaranteed good employment, and the main function of the degree was "a way for the merchant elite to distinguish their sons in society,"[104] higher education was essentially a luxury good. As such, heavy investments were made in beautiful and lavish campuses, college sports, and so forth, so much so that only twenty-one cents of every tuition dollar is actually spent on instruction![105] These things represent a massive cost burden on institutions as they struggle to adapt to the new landscape. That's why colleges that charged you six figures for your education routinely call you for donations. (For a showcase on the absurdity of that situation, do a Google search for "John Mulaney Majoring in English.")

> Only twenty-one cents of every tuition dollar is actually spent on instruction!

This last strike against higher education is particularly telling because while everything else could be overcome, there's a final nail in higher education's coffin that most incumbents don't face: money. Understanding this last part will take a detour, but it's an important detour, because the economics of higher education will be the ultimate deciding factor.

CONSOLIDATION: WHEN INDUSTRIES COME TOGETHER

In 1983, the ownership of 90 percent of American media was split across fifty companies. By 2012, that number was down to six media giants that control 90 percent of what Americans read, watch, and listen to: Comcast, which owns NBC, Universal Pictures, and Focus Features; NewsCorp, with Fox, the *New York Post,* and the *Wall Street Journal,* which later was later acquired by Amazon founder Jeff Bezos; Disney, with ABC, ESPN, and Pixar; Viacom, with MTV, Nickelodeon, and Paramount Pictures; Time Warner, with CNN, HBO, and TIME; and CBS, with its namesake channel CBS, Showtime, and the Smithsonian channel.

This pattern of consolidation can be seen in industry after industry. Some big companies regroup to make a few even bigger ones, like the "big nine" accounting firms in 1986 consolidating into the "big four" by the early 2000s.[106] An emerging market leader may leave everyone else falling by the wayside, like Google in search engines. Bing is a distant second, and most people don't remember competitors like AltaVista, Lycos, or Mamma. At the top of some industries you'll find a handful of giants—think aircraft manufacturers, telecom, or big consulting. In some markets there may be a single "winner takes most" structure in which one player owns the lion's share, and the rest is spread among a handful of also-rans—think Netflix vs. Hulu and Amazon in streaming video, Uber vs. Lyft in ride sharing, or Facebook and LinkedIn vs. everything else in social networking.

ONE PLUS ONE EQUALS MORE THAN TWO

Consolidation generally happens in situations where one plus one adds up to more than two, for example, in the case of a couple coming together to start a family. There are many things that I can do alone, and the same is true of my wife, but to have children, we need each other. In our case, one plus one added up to four.

The same principle operates on the scale of industries. If twenty companies can each invest a million dollars toward solving a problem, and the twenty-first company can invest twenty million dollars to solve the same problem, the last company has a clear advantage. The math in favor of consolidation is even stronger because there are also efficiencies to gain and replicated efforts to reduce. The resulting resources can be reinvested in the solution or passed on to the customer as savings. This will be true as long as the total of consumers and consumer dollars is large enough to justify the size of the agglomeration. In other words, when enough people want and need the same thing for such a large entity to make sense of providing it.

AND THE RICH GET RICHER

Finally, there's the flywheel effect of the rich getting richer. Compare the typical American (median net worth of $44,900[107]) with Warren Buffett (net worth upwards of $80 billion). Let's assume both can invest the entirety of their net worth, and let's take Buffett's extraordinary investing skill out of the equation by promising both him and the average American the same percentage return of eight percent per year. In one year the average American's net worth will grow by more than $3,592. That's not too shabby until you consider that in the same time and with the same proportional allocation of resources, Mr. Buffett's net worth will grow by more than $6 billion! Return is a function of investment, and the more you can put in, the more you stand to take out.

This is why so many industries start with a "land grab" of companies racing to "get big fast"—a mantra that was taken to extremes in the days of the dot com bubble—because once you start getting a lead on the competition, that lead tends to compound itself. Imagine, for example, that you come onto the scene with search technology every bit as good as Google's. Even with you and Google at the same starting line, you're moving only as fast as you can innovate on your own, while Google is propelled by the combined efforts of thousands of engineers.

So industries consolidate when economies of scale can make one plus one add up to more than two, and companies can gain advantages by pooling resources and turning the flywheel on an existing lead to get even further ahead. Much of this logic applies to the world of education.

THE CONSOLIDATION OF FOUNDATIONAL, "LAST MILE," AND POPULAR CONTINUING EDUCATION

Almost every one of the thousands of universities and colleges in the United States and around the world offers a Psychology 101 course, and the same is true in almost every area of study. Introductory courses often are delivered in auditoriums that hold hundreds of students, and most of the interaction and feedback is provided by teaching assistants. Does it really make sense for thousands of professors with varying levels of teaching ability delivering the same course when it can be done once by the best teacher in the world, as is the vision of MOOCs like Coursera?

This math won't work in every situation, but it fits well with the sort of education and training that lots of people need. This is true of foundational education that everyone requires, "last mile" education into popular career paths, and the most popular continuing education courses. While the catalog of possible courses is enormous, currently a third of all course credits earned in American bachelor's degrees are in only thirty courses,[108] which have a mainstream enough appeal to fit with consolidation. In all those cases, a huge number of people need the same thing, and there is much to be gained by offering a single best-in-class solution rather than a large variety of mediocre ones.

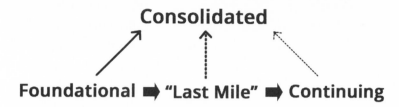

Consolidated

Foundational ➡ **"Last Mile"** ➡ **Continuing**

Remember that consolidation happens when one plus one equals more than two, which is in situations where synergies and efficiencies allow for resources to be better deployed by one big organization than by many small ones. It also occurs when there is a large enough market of people who want the same thing. This sort of education will be consolidated into a relatively small number of providers. There are three places these providers could emerge: top universities, staffing firms, and upstarts.

Top universities. If I had to bet on one place that today's universities will grow into, it is offering mainstream foundational education and perhaps popular continuing education classes. After all, that's what they strive to do today, albeit not very successfully. There won't be many winners because that's how consolidation works. Also, it will be a scary proposition for colleges to undertake. Since part of the value of their signal comes from its scarcity, they risk the commoditization and cannibalization of offering it on a mainstream basis. In other words, while courses from top schools like Harvard, MIT, Stanford, and others are available online at low or no cost, the value of degrees from those institutions would plummet if anyone could get them that easily. However, their name recognition and reputation give them a significant advantage, and they have the financial wherewithal to take risks: the five richest schools alone each have endowments ranging from $22 billion to $38 billion.[109] Each is larger than the gross domestic product of almost half the countries of the world, and in combination more than the GDP of Morocco (population 35 million) or the Ukraine (population 45 million).[110] That's enough money to pay for a lot of risk taking and experimentation, if leadership has the stomach for it.

Staffing firms. The second likely candidate from which "last mile" education in particular is likely to come is staffing firms. Staffing was a $428 billion industry globally in 2016,[111] with market leaders like Adecco, Randstad, and ManpowerGroup earning in the range of $20 billion each year. Their revenues are directly correlated with their ability to find and place skilled people, and the skilled worker shortage in the United States alone could be worth many tens of billions of dollars to them, so their motivation will be strong. Unlike the incumbents of higher education, they have nothing to lose by entering this space with mainstream training. But on the other hand, this does mean a significant step beyond their current scope of focus, which requires vision, can feel risky, and depends on the development of expertise that they don't currently have.

Upstarts. This is the mystery door number three. We can guess at which incumbents have the resources and vantage point with the best chance of cashing in on an impending disruption, just like William Durant, whose position as a titan of the horse-drawn carriage industry set him up well to start General Motors. However, history has taught us that innovation usually comes from the outside, seemingly out of nowhere. That's how it was as far back as Henry Ford and as recently as Tesla's Elon Musk. Although the odds of any particular innovator beating the incumbent are slim, the odds of the incumbent being beaten by innovators are strong. There are many start-ups working today to disrupt and innovate the space of education, including my company Mirasee and others that I'll share with you. There are even venture capital funds[112] dedicated to this opportunity. Probably the best final words when it comes to the future of mainstream education are "watch this space."

We can expect a large part of the educational landscape to be concentrated into a small number of top providers, and I've shared my best guesses as to where those providers are likely to emerge. But that's only half the story because just as parts of the education landscape consolidate, others break apart.

DID YOU GET ALL THAT? (LEARNING SELF-ASSESSMENT)

Want to test your understanding of the ideas that we just covered? Or start conversations with interested friends and colleagues? Here are a few questions to guide you:

1. Where does innovation usually come from: inside an industry, or elsewhere?

2. What are the two big advantages of incumbency?

3. Why are incumbents less likely to embrace change and innovation?

4. What are the major anchors and blinders hampering today's colleges/universities from innovating?

5. Universities do double duty as both teaching and research institutions. How does this get in the way of effective teaching?

6. How do the laws of tenure constrain education?

7. What conditions set the stage for consolidation, and how do those conditions apply to higher education?

8. Who are the three most plausible categories of providers of consolidated foundational or "last mile" education?

9. What do staffing firms have at stake in improving higher education?

10. What are some of the signs that startups are disrupting and innovating in the space of education?

LIKE WHAT YOU READ, AND WANT TO GO DEEPER?

Here are a few good books to take a look at if you'd like to go deeper on some of the ideas presented in this chapter.

- Ryan Craig's *College Disrupted* and *A New U*

For more information, including this entire book in digital format plus actionable conversation video guides at the end of each chapter, an expanded and up-to-date bibliography, and additional resources, visit LeveragedLearningBook.com

CHAPTER 5

Learning from the Experts

S CIENCE FICTION fans in the early 1970s had slim pickings. There were some movies, novels, and three seasons of the original *Star Trek*. The first San Diego Comic-Con was held in August 1970, with roughly 300 attendees flocking to hear guests like Ray Bradbury, Jack Kirby, and A. E. van Vogt.

Fast forward a few decades, and sci-fi fans are blessed with a cornucopia of choices, including *Star Trek* franchise spinoffs; *Star Wars* sequels and prequels; the *Marvel Comic* and *Harry Potter* universes; movie series like *The Matrix* and *Terminator*; television shows like *The Twilight Zone*, *The X-Files*, *Doctor Who*, and *Battlestar Galactica*; movies that turned into television shows like *Stargate*; and even aborted cult series like *Firefly* and Netflix's recent *Sense8*. And it's not only about choosing media, but also about choosing sides, with rivalries like *Star Trek* vs. *Star Wars*, or *Deep Space Nine* vs. *Babylon 5*, and *X-Men* vs. *The Avengers*. There's even *Galaxy Quest*, a parody of the tropes turning up in all the rest. Not to mention Comic-Con, the annual conference attended by over a hundred thousand fans. Far from consolidating, this industry has exploded into smithereens!

This is instructive, because we see the same pattern in the world of education; just as some parts of industry consolidate, others are breaking apart. Let's explore what leads to this fragmentation, and what it means for education.

FRAGMENTATION: WHEN INDUSTRIES BREAK APART

Sometimes industries don't consolidate. In fact, sometimes they break into more and more pieces. Let's return to the media landscape that we looked at in the last chapter. It is an interesting study in contrasts. At the same time as fifty media companies agglomerated into just six, the choice among just three television networks (ABC, CBS, and NBC) expanded to an average of one hundred eight-nine channels available and seventeen watched in the average American home in 2014,[113] not to mention all the programming that is available on Netflix, Hulu, and YouTube!

The classic example of this pattern of fragmentation is the book industry. In the days of Abraham Lincoln, one was lucky to have the opportunity to read a few dozen books in a lifetime, and the total of books available was numbered in the thousands or tens of thousands. The pace of book production grew to almost ten thousand new books per year in the early 1900s, and it continued to climb as high as three million new books per year in 2010.[114] Of course, these numbers are cumulative; in 2010 Google reported almost one hundred thirty million books in existence,[115] of which fifteen thousand were about Lincoln![116]

MULTIPLE (NON-EXCLUSIVE) WAYS TO WIN

The first thing required for fragmentation to happen is more than one way to win. This is sometimes a function of utility; when it comes to pounding a nail into the wall, a hammer is a hammer is a hammer. The same isn't true of screwdrivers, though: There are flat heads, Phillips heads, the rarer square head, and the Torx head, which is shaped like a six-pointed star). More often, though, fragmentation is a function of taste. While there's just one way to hammer a nail, there are infinite ways to write a novel, compose a song, plan a great vacation, or prepare tomato sauce, which is why your local grocery store offers an array of flavors like sweet basil marinara, sun-dried tomato, Florentine spinach and cheese, tomato and pesto, tomato Alfredo, and many more.

In other words, we're looking for situations where one choice doesn't exclude you (or somebody else) from also making another. This is true in industries like music, where listening to one song or artist doesn't preclude people from listening to many others; fashion, where I can own many different shirts from many brands, and so can you; tourism, as vacationing in London doesn't preclude us from also vacationing in Cancun; apps, since installing Waze on my phone doesn't preclude me from also installing Slack, Spotify, or Angry Birds; and even cars, as I may not be in the market for more than one, but my driving a Toyota doesn't preclude you from buying something else. Of course, this is also true in the book industry; buying and reading one book doesn't preclude you from buying and reading another, a fact for which I as an author am grateful!

LOW BARRIERS TO ENTRY

Sometimes the operative constraint isn't in what people want (demand), but rather in what can be provided (supply). Even if there were an unlimited number of good ways to design an airplane, for example (which the laws of aerodynamics suggest there aren't), the enormous cost of producing an airplane combined with the relatively low number of buyers (essentially just airlines, freight companies, and very wealthy individuals) means that there isn't room in the market for a whole lot of options.

Returning to books, the explosion of available titles occurs not because so many more people want to read books, but rather because it's so much easier for authors to write and publish them. The same is true for musicians, app developers, video producers, and so forth. Where the means of production were once expensive and scarce, they're now cheap and accessible.

ENTER LONG TAIL ECONOMICS

This combination of multiple non-exclusive ways to win and a market with low barriers to entry for new players can create myriad options, with a unique set of economic properties that Chris Anderson described in his 2004 article in *Wired* magazine titled "The Long Tail" and his 2006 book by the same name. The "long tail" is a simple concept with powerful implications. Here it is in a nutshell, as articulated by Anderson on his website:

> ...our culture and economy is increasingly shifting away from a focus on a relatively small number of 'hits' (mainstream products and markets) at the head of the demand curve and toward a huge number of niches in the tail. As the costs of production and distribution fall, especially online, there is now less need to lump products and consumers into one-size-fits-all containers. In an era without the constraints of physical shelf space and other bottlenecks of distribution, narrowly targeted goods and services can be as economically attractive as mainstream fare.[117]

In other words, shelf space in brick-and-mortar stores was a limited commodity; with only so much room, they stocked only stuff that they knew a lot of people would buy (the "hits"). When stores went digital, and the concept of shelf space became meaningless, it let all the "non-hits" into the market for those who wanted them. This is fantastic for all those whose tastes don't conform to top forty lists in every category!

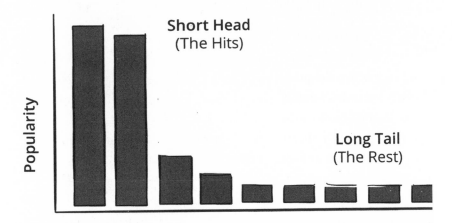

In aggregate, the yield of long-tail marketplaces can be spectacular; sites like Amazon and iTunes see a substantial portion of their traffic and revenue come from the long tail of titles that most of us have never even heard of. However, this works only because of the immense quantity of those titles; for the artists and producers who live in the long tail, the returns are dismal. Everybody knows about the hits, but hardly anyone has heard of the rest. This is true of YouTube video producers (a third of videos published on YouTube have fewer than ten views), app developers (94 percent of the revenue in the Apple App Store comes from just one percent of all publishers, and 60 percent of apps go un-downloaded), authors on Kindle (the vast majority sell less than a hundred books), and so on. Because these platforms rely on volume to succeed, they tend to force pricing models that are great for the hits, but not for everyone else. That's why success with most opportunities that rely on long-tail economics requires that you move large quantities of inventory on a monthly, weekly, or even daily basis.

Now that we understand how markets fragment, let's turn our attention back to the topic at hand. We've already seen which parts of the education industry will consolidate, so now let's see which parts will break apart.

THE UNLIKELY SOURCE OF "LAST MILE" EDUCATION AND LIFELONG LEARNING

Foundational education will come from a few select providers, and the same is true of major "last mile" trainings and the most popular of continuing education courses. That's the stuff at the fat head, but what about the long tail? This where the bulk of the education we consume over our lifetimes will come from—short and focused courses delivering just the information, insight, and fortitude that we need, just when we need it. This will include more niche-focused "last mile" education, and the majority of continuing education courses on a plethora of topics. Before we learn where this education will come from, let's understand why it *can't* come from today's universities and colleges.

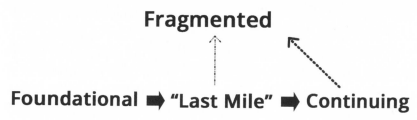

Colleges are unlikely to evolve in this direction for all the reasons that make innovation challenging, which we explored in the last chapter. The biggest reason it isn't going to happen, though, is money: There's just no way that they can afford it. Here's why: Of all the challenges and inefficiencies of mainstream higher education today, its ace in the hole has been that education comes in a bundle of at least two years, and usually four. This means that colleges' vast catalogs of courses, most of which are at advanced or graduate levels usually attended by small numbers of people, historically have been subsidized by the massively attended introductory courses that are mandatory for undergraduates starting their programs. This is doubly true (or rather, five times as true, if you do the math) when you consider that only 21 cents of every tuition dollar actually goes to instruction![118]

We've seen this pattern before, for example with cable companies making us pay for all sorts of channels that we don't watch in order to get access to the few that we do. Right now, college works the same way, a fact which won't be true for much longer. The unbundling of courses from each other and from the college experience as a whole will be devastating to these institutions, as Ryan Craig explains: "For higher education, unbundling would drastically reduce revenue per student. As a result, the cost structure of colleges and universities would need to downshift dramatically."[119] All this comes against the backdrop of an education bubble that is popping slowly, at which point public confidence and the enrollment revenue it has driven into institutions of higher learning will drop precipitously. So try as they might, colleges just won't be able to play in this arena. The math just doesn't work.

For higher education, unbundling would drastically reduce revenue per student.

If not colleges, who will provide the lifelong learning of the future? From the only place that it can come from: the experts and professionals on the cutting edge and front lines of their respective fields. They're the only ones whose knowledge and skills will be sufficiently up to date to provide what learners will need. While their skill level and opportunity cost will command a premium, the transformation that they will deliver will justify paying it. Some colleges see the writing on the wall, and are scrambling to hire these very experts as "adjunct professors." This is great proof of concept for the experts, but only a band-aid for the colleges; they're still hampered from evolving by all the factors that we've explored, and experts are already realizing that they have more freedom to innovate and to earn meaningful income without being tied to a university.

WHY WE NEED TO LEARN FROM EXPERTS FIRST AND TEACHERS SECOND

In 1451, an Italian notary named Ser Piero had an affair with a peasant woman named Caterina, and nine months later she bore him a son. Formal schooling was out of the question for an illegitimate child, but Ser Piero wanted his son to find a stable profession. He noticed that the boy had a talent for drawing, and when the boy turned 14, his father arranged for him to apprentice in the workshop of Andrea di Cione, known as Verrocchio, which was considered to be one of the finest painters in Florence. The boy was Leonardo da Vinci.

The apprenticeship model, in which a student studies directly under a practicing master, is common in human history. This would seem to make sense. Who better to learn from than someone actually doing what you're seeking to learn, on the front lines of the trade? Wouldn't a practitioner be the obvious choice over an educator or academic any day of the week?

Actually, no. There are good reasons why a teacher would be a better choice than a practitioner, the most important being that teaching is hard. It takes patience to move at the students' pace, skill to reach them where they are, and imagination to understand how things look from their point of view and to find metaphors and examples that help them reach the appropriate conclusions. Teaching is an art and a science, and expecting that being a practitioner of a skill automatically translates to being able to teach it simply isn't reasonable. Expecting a chess master to be good at teaching chess is a bit like expecting an athlete to be a good coach. Playing chess and being good at basketball are fundamentally different skills from teaching and coaching. Reality is the *opposite* of the trope: "Those who can, do. Those who can't, teach." Good teachers are the ones who can, and do, and teach, but that intersection can be a difficult balancing act.

> Good teachers are the ones who can, and do, and teach—but that intersection can be a difficult balancing act.

The question of subject matter knowledge vs. teaching skill isn't "Which is more important?" (you need both), but rather "Which is harder to develop?" Since most of the history of formal education was characterized by a fairly static curriculum, the answer was the teaching skill. Whether it took a few months to master your times tables in elementary school or a few years to master trigonometry in college, once you got it, you had it. Neither the times tables nor trigonometry are changing anytime soon. The same is true for most topics, whether it's double-entry bookkeeping, the history of medieval Europe, or the correct form for doing a push-up. The subject matter involved in the job remained static or changed slowly enough that an occasional conference or continuing education course was enough to stay up to date. The rest of the teacher's time and energy could be devoted to improving their craft of teaching and actually working with students.

But the pace of change has increased, and rapidly, to the point that everything we learn is obsolete within five to ten years. This dramatically changes the game of staying up to date, such that the only practical way to remain as current as needed is to be in the trenches and on the front lines, actually doing the work and learning on the job. This pace of change has necessitated that our priorities shift; while the best choice of educator used to be a great teacher who also knew the subject matter, now the only ones who can do the job are the experts in subject matter who are also great teachers.

BUT WHICH EXPERTS?

Imagine for a moment that you're the literally most powerful man in the world, and your teenage son needs a tutor. Whom do you get to do the job? In 343 BCE, this wasn't a hypothetical question. King Philip II of Macedonia needed a tutor for his 13-year-old son, so he summoned the leading thinker of his day to be his son's tutor. The thinker's name was Aristotle, and the student's name was Alexander, who grew to become Alexander the Great.

From the king's vantage point, this makes perfect sense. You want the very best for your child, and you have the resources and authority to make a compelling case to one of the greatest philosophers in history. The role looked good from Aristotle's vantage point as well; one imagines that tutor to the crown prince would be a pretty good gig. And besides, what else was he going to do?

But modern learners don't have the resources or authority of King Philip II, and today's experts have more and better options to choose from than Aristotle did in 343 BCE. The modern equivalent of being tutored by Aristotle might be private instruction on writing with Malcolm Gladwell and James Patterson, filmmaking with Ron Howard and Martin Scorsese, photography with Annie Leibovitz, singing and performance with Christina Aguilera and Usher, cooking with Gordon Ramsay, and chess with Garry Kasparov. They are all leaders in their respective fields and are motivated to share their knowledge by filming a video course for the MasterClass platform, which includes a few dozen videos and even a handful of group Q&A calls with the expert. That's great, but it's not a private tutoring relationship, any more than reading *The Complete Works of Aristotle* can be equated to the learning experience of Alexander the Great.

This isn't a criticism of the great video courses that these experts have recorded, but rather a recognition that what they offer is akin to reading a book that happens to be in video format. It's not the sort of transformation that direct access or apprenticeship would create. There's no other way that this could be, for two big reasons:

- **Reason 1: Logistics.** There is only one of each of these experts and potentially millions who would want to learn at their feet.

- **Reason 2: Opportunity cost.** Even if they could directly instruct each person who wanted to learn from them, they're too busy tending to their day jobs of making movies, composing hit songs, and running restaurants.

You might be able to get around these reasons if you're the modern equivalent of the king of Macedonia, but otherwise you'll have to look elsewhere for continuing education. We look one rung down the ladder, to the experts and professionals at the top of their game and the forefront of their field, who haven't yet written *New York Times* best-selling books, produced award-winning reality TV shows, or famously beaten every human opponent on the planet only to fall eventually fall to IBM's Deep Blue supercomputer. Those experts alone have the combination of cutting-edge knowledge and skills, exposure to work that allows them to maintain their edge, and opportunity cost that means earning extra tens of thousands, hundreds of thousands, or on rare occasions millions of dollars a year is well worth their while.

Of course, we prefer the subset of those experts who also have either the ability or the potential to be great teachers. They are the ones who will supply the highly fragmented demand for some "last mile" education and most of the continuing education courses that we as a society will need to stay current.

Pausing to reflect, we've come a long way together. In the first half of this book, we've explored why education in its present form is failing us, what it needs to do to carry us into the future, and where we can expect that new education to emerge. The next half of the book will be dedicated to what education will need to look like to get us where we need to go, and how we will go about creating it.

DID YOU GET ALL THAT?
(LEARNING SELF-ASSESSMENT)

Want to test your understanding of the ideas that we just covered? Or start conversations with interested friends and colleagues? Here are a few questions to guide you:

1. What is fragmentation as it applies to business?

2. What are the conditions that lead to the fragmentation of a market or industry?

3. What does Chris Anderson mean by "the long tail"?

4. Will the education market move towards consolidation or fragmentation?

5. Why can't continuing education come from today's universities and colleges?

6. Why is the bulk of the continuing education market likely to become fragmented?

7. Why does it make more sense to learn from a good teacher than from a practitioner?

8. Everything we learn becomes obsolete in 5-10 years. How does this impact continuing education?

9. Is it better to learn from a great teacher or from a subject matter expert?

10. Who will be the best providers of continuing education courses?

LIKE WHAT YOU READ, AND WANT TO GO DEEPER?

Here are a few good books to take a look at if you'd like to go deeper on some of the ideas presented in this chapter.

- Jeff Cobb's *Leading the Learning Revolution*

- My own book, *Teach and Grow Rich*

For more information, including this entire book in digital format plus actionable conversation video guides at the end of each chapter, an expanded and up-to-date bibliography, and additional resources, visit LeveragedLearningBook.com

And if you'd like to put out your own shingle as an educator entrepreneur, a good place to start is to join one of the free Course Building Bootcamps offered by my company Mirasee; details at LeveragedLearning.co/cbb.

PART 2

What is Leveraged Learning, and How To Do It

(The Components of World-Class Education)

CHAPTER 6

Knowledge: Making it Easy for People to Learn

Just how quickly can you learn skills such as surfing, professional poker, Brazilian jujitsu, parkour, or foreign languages? The education system needs to teach in the most effective ways. It needs to use what science has taught us about how people learn to engage learners in rapid skill development. Lectures have long been known as a poor way to bring people up to speed. But what works instead? To find out, let's look at how people learn.

There's a subculture of meta-learning and rapid skill acquisition dedicated to answering these questions, popularized by Timothy Ferriss in his *4-Hour* book series, podcast, and television show. Connor Grooms is one of those rapid learning aficionados. After running several thirty-day experiments with goals including learning web design, making films, and even putting on twenty-six pounds of muscle, Grooms turned his attention to learning Spanish. He not only learned to speak Spanish, but also made a documentary about the process.[120] Grooms worked hard to get so good so quickly, investing five hours a day for thirty days while maintaining his full-time work. Writing for *Forbes,* Jared Kleinert explained Grooms' process:

His success lies in finding the learning methods that work best from a data-driven approach, whether traditional (like flashcards) or unconventional (like a mimicking method he follows in the documentary to learn proper pronunciation). Nothing Grooms does is absurd. He's simply willing to take advice from dozens of books, world-class mentors like Benny Lewis when it comes to language-learning, and then actually put in the work.[121]

This rapid learning experiment formed the basis of what eventually became BaseLang, Grooms' Spanish tutoring company, which Kleinert described as "the closest thing to immersion you can get without moving to a Spanish-speaking country." Not one to rest on his laurels, Grooms decided to raise the ante on how quickly languages can be learned. He enlisted the help of Tony Marsh, a language teacher whose clients include the U.S. Navy and NATO, to learn Portuguese in just a week.[122]

Here's the thing about learning a language, whether it's Spanish, Portuguese, or anything else: fluency alone doesn't qualify you to do all that much. On the other hand, the *lack* of fluency can disqualify you from a whole lot! The same is true of most knowledge and skills, unless they're highly specialized, or you reach a top-tier level of proficiency. For example, a basic fluency in the skill of cooking might qualify you to prepare dinner for your family, but to work in the field you'll have to kick things up several notches. The same goes for everything from management to martial arts. A basic conceptual fluency doesn't actually get you all that far. The key to real value is in the ability to do great things with your knowledge.

The key to real value is in the ability to do great things with your knowledge.

With that said, we do still need the knowledge. It isn't the be all and end all, but it is the foundation for any success that we care to achieve. So it makes sense for us to follow Grooms' lead and acquire the knowledge that we need as quickly and efficiently as possible, in order to move on to bigger and better things. Entire excellent books have been written on this field, and I couldn't hope to give it an exhaustive treatment in a single chapter. What follows is the bare minimum that you need to know and understand in order to do this well, starting with why learning and memory are so hard.

To understand how we might accelerate the learning process in this way, let's turn our attention to memory, which is the base building unit of learning.

WHY LEARNING AND MEMORY ARE SO HARD

Imagine a spectrum of all the things you might learn. On one end you'll find something like remembering your phone number or reciting the *Gettysburg Address*—that's knowledge acquisition, pure and simple, with no skill involved. Learning professionals call this *declarative memory*, which is the "knowing what" of vocabulary, theories, dates, facts, and figures. On the other end is something like tying your shoelace or riding a bicycle. That's pure skill, and there's really no informational knowledge required. This is called *procedural memory*, which is the "knowing how" to do things, generally involving motor skills. Of course, there are lots of things that sit somewhere in the middle and call on both types of memory, like playing tennis, driving a car, negotiating a deal, baking an apple pie, or preparing a budget.[123]

Declarative Memory   **Procedural Memory**

All of these things are based on remembering and repeating (either in words or in actions) the things that we've been told and shown. That sounds easy, but it isn't. It turns out that remembering is surprisingly hard.

OUR BRAINS ARE DESIGNED TO FORGET

Sir Arthur Conan Doyle's Sherlock Holmes is more than the epitome of deductive brilliance, he also presents a fascinating insight into how we all think and how we might think better. One of Holmes' famous eccentricities was a deep and thorough knowledge of some areas, and a striking lack of knowledge of others. When taken to task for this by his sidekick, Dr. John Watson, in *A Study in Scarlet*, Holmes explains, "I consider that a man's brain originally is like a little empty attic, and you have to stock it with such furniture as you choose."[124] Essentially, Holmes is saying that he's careful to *not* learn certain things, in order to make room for the things that he deems truly important to know.

While Holmes may be extreme, he is far from unique. We are all exposed to far more information than we can notice or retain, and our brains aren't designed to remember everything that we've ever learned. In fact, they're designed to retain only what they actually need, which means that memories evaporate entirely over time if not used. So when we forget huge chunks of things that we used to know, it isn't necessarily evidence of laziness or attention deficits, but rather a sign that our brains are working exactly as they should.[125] In other words, the challenge of retention isn't a bug, it's a feature, albeit a sometimes annoying one.

> The challenge of retention isn't a bug, it's a feature—albeit a sometimes annoying one.

How do our brains decide whether knowledge or skill is worthy of being remembered? There are a few criteria, the first of which is whether we understand it in the first place.

SCAFFOLDING IDEAS ON TOP OF IDEAS

Computers can run millions of calculations in a matter of moments, but they can't actually think, or know, or understand. That's a good thing if you're looking to program them to do something new: You don't have to explain why it makes sense or think about tying your idea to their existing knowledge base. You just write the software, and the computer runs it. Easy peasy. With human beings, it's decidedly more complicated. Our brains aren't designed to assimilate information and ideas completely unrelated to our context or frame of reference. Anything we learn or are exposed to must fit somewhere in the hierarchy of the things that we already know and understand.

That's why so much of the art of teaching and explaining is finding the metaphors and telling the stories that help students connect new ideas to things that they already know. Learning professionals call this *scaffolding*—building one idea on top of another—and it's why this book is laden with stories and vignettes. Hopefully, they help you get your head around the ideas I'm presenting and entertain you along the way.

The lack of scaffolding is one of the biggest reasons why learning breaks down, and conversely it is the reason why some remediation programs have impressive results. Consider, for example, reading interventions for children who are severely below grade level, which can effectively advance participants by several grade levels in a few months.[126] They're great programs, but they beg the question of why we couldn't have applied them to all the kids in the class to begin with and saved them years of study. The answer is that in many cases, remediation works not only because of the extra attention and excellent pedagogy, but also because in the years between the original learning attempts and remediation, the necessary scaffolding of supporting concepts and ideas was built.

> Lack of scaffolding is one of the biggest reasons why learning breaks down.

Note also that scaffolding can sometimes be a function of development and maturity, in addition to prior learning. In other words, some thing (like quantum physics) are hard no matter how old or smart you are. But other things (like basic addition) are hard up until a certain developmental maturity has been reached, and then they become easy. This is one of the challenges for people possessing what Todd Rose calls "jagged learning profiles"—stronger in some areas and weaker in others.

We're all some configuration of jagged, and expecting us all to progress at the same pace in all areas makes very little sense.

Without scaffolding, it's hard to make sense of what you're learning, and rule number one of memory is that if we don't understand it, we don't remember it. And rule number two? That has to do with how relevant the information is to you.

INFERRING RELEVANCE FROM THE CONE OF EXPERIENCE

Born in 1900 in Minnesota, Edgar Dale showed passion for effective education ranging from vocabulary to readability to his doctoral thesis, titled *Factual Basis for Curriculum Revision in Arithmetic with Special Reference to Children's Understanding of Business Terms*. At the age of 46, Dale developed a concept called the Cone of Experience in a textbook on audiovisual methods in teaching.[127]

That model has been widely misrepresented as the Cone of Learning, which purports to say how much people remember based on how information is presented to them (from 10 percent of what we read and 20 percent of what we hear, to 70 percent of what we say and write, and 90 percent of what we do). Now, this is layer upon layer of bad science. Dale's original Cone of Experience was not based on scientific research, and he even warned his readers not to take it too seriously. And the retention percentages weren't even part of his original diagram. They were added later on.

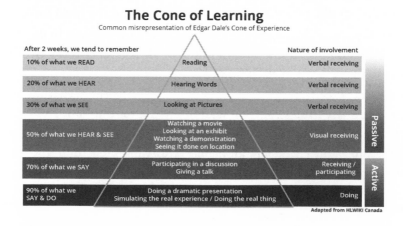

The Cone of Learning

Common misrepresentation of Edgar Dale's Cone of Experience

Treating this model as gospel would be an egregious overreaching, as would giving any weight to the specific numbers on the diagram. But even though the model is sorely lacking in factual accuracy, it is directionally correct and useful. It intuitively makes sense to us that we would better remember something that we actually did than something that we read in passing in a book.

This is for two reasons: The first is that learning is associative. In other words, memories are linked to the environment, experience, and state of mind in which they were formed. There is ample research showing that this is true, ranging from divers who memorized words while underwater and were better able to recall those words underwater than on land, students who memorized words while jazz music was playing and were better able to remember them with jazz music than without, and bipolar patients who best remembered things they experienced during manic phases when they were again in manic phases, and likewise for depressive phases.[128]

Memories are linked to the environment, experience, and state of mind in which they were formed.

The second reason is pragmatic. We remember what our brains think is relevant to us, and the more involved we are with the experience (doing, discussing, and writing, as opposed to reading, hearing, and seeing), the more likely it is to be relevant to us.

So far our whirlwind tour of how we learn and form memories has taken us through the two types of memory, our natural tendencies to forget, scaffolding concepts on top of others, and the need for learning experiences that tell our brains the material is relevant to us. We'll explore how to design all this into a learning experience soon. But first, there's one more important factor to consider, which is that often even if we do remember, it doesn't mean we've really learned what we were hoping to learn.

GOOD LEARNING,
AKA WHY KARATE KID DOESN'T WORK

"Wax on, wax off" has become a cultural catchphrase, synonymous with karate instruction, learning by doing, and the movie that started it all. The original 1984 *Karate Kid* tells the tale of Daniel LaRusso, a scrawny kid from New Jersey who moves to Southern California. He runs afoul of a group of boys who study a predatory brand of karate called Cobra Kai, whose motto is "Strike first, strike hard, no mercy." LaRusso meets Mr. Miyagi, a wise old man who teaches the boy his own brand of karate, which emphasizes self-defense and inner balance.

The training follows a non-traditional approach. While his Cobra Kai rivals practice punching and kicking in their dojo, Mr. Miyagi demands obedience from LaRusso with no questions asked and sets him to perform tasks such as sanding the floor, painting the fence, and waxing his cars (the iconic "wax on, wax off"). Finally LaRusso's patience with seemingly pointless manual labor wears thin, and he challenges Miyagi to stop wasting his time. In the scene where it all comes to a head, Miyagi unleashes a flurry of punches and kicks that LaRusso surprises himself by blocking, using the movements he had practiced for sanding the floor, painting the fence, and so on.

It's one of the movie's classic moments, marking the start of LaRusso's transformation from a wimpy, anxious kid to a competent, capable *karateka* who has found his center. There's just one problem with the whole story: In real life, it never would have worked.

The idea of extrapolating the ability to block a punch from the experience of waxing a car is an example of what learning professionals call *far transfer* (as opposed to *near transfer*, which might be the ability to wax other cars or maybe boats). Far transfer, the ability to apply relevant learning to unfamiliar situations, is the holy grail of education. As Howard Gardner, the developmental psychologist behind the theory of multiple intelligences, writes, "An individual understands a concept, skill, theory, or domain of knowledge to the extent that he or she can apply it appropriately in a new situation."[129]

> To achieve far transfer, we must not only teach the relevant underlying principles, but also help students see how they apply in a wide range of circumstances.

This is easier said than done. To achieve far transfer, we must not only teach the relevant underlying principles, but also help students see how they apply in a wide range of circumstances.[130] This doesn't happen automagically, as *Karate Kid* suggests. Joseph Aoun, president of Northeastern University in Boston, explains this further:

> Studies have shown that students rarely exhibit the ability to apply relevant learning to unfamiliar situations. They may find themselves overly dependent on familiar contexts and inflexible to new applications. They also may lack a deep understanding of their domain, knowing the what but not the why. This blinds them from seeing how their knowledge could be utilized in a different setting.[131]

How can we engineer learning that is effective and efficient, that creates useful far transfer, and that sticks? It's a tall order, but thankfully there are some shortcuts to get there.

FIRST, BUILD YOUR SCAFFOLDING

Imagine that you have to change a light bulb, but you can't reach the fixture in the ceiling. The smart thing to do is get a ladder, but maybe the ladder is behind a small mountain of knickknacks in the garage, or maybe you don't have a ladder and must trek across town to get one. So you place a barstool under the fixture and a chair on top of the bar stool. Because the fixture is still just out of reach, you grab a pair of salad tongs for the extra few inches. Armed with the salad tongs, you carefully climb on the chair that teeters atop the barstool and slowly reach up with the salad tongs, praying that you can maintain your balance long enough to accomplish the task before the whole thing comes tumbling down.

It sounds absurd, but this is precisely what far too many instructors attempt with their students and why so much learning never happens. Before designing a curriculum, instructors must ask themselves what knowledge and skill are prerequisites to the learning and whether it is realistic to expect the entire student base to be prepared. If the answer is no, the prerequisites must be built into the learning process. Minerva Schools at KGI, for example, offer a unique scaffolded program that progresses from being almost completely structured in the first year, to being almost completely driven by the students themselves in the fourth year.[132] This is designed to give students the skills that they need to successfully tackle the later material.

There are many ways to do this effectively. Take, for example, the concept of a "memory palace."[133] The idea is to create imaginary locations in your mind where you can store mnemonic images. The most common type of memory palace involves making a journey through a place you know well, like a building or town. Along that journey there are specific locations that you always visit in the same order. This is literally a process of building visual imagery as scaffolding to support learning, in a context where you don't have other scaffolding to hook new ideas onto. Another common practice is priming new learning by explaining how and why it will be used. This creates meaning that connects new learning to existing context, which all comes down to scaffolding.

Abstract concepts especially require scaffolding. Our brains aren't wired to think abstractly, and our workaround involves analogies and metaphors. Einstein, for example, postulated his theories of physics by imagining the relative speed of a man walking on a moving train. Similarly, when we think of a timeline, we tend to imagine them in a visual order. These are metaphors that allow us to think about things our brains weren't wired to think about.

So scaffolding is key, but it's only the first of two. With solid scaffolding firmly in place, you're ready to encode the new knowledge or skill.

SECOND, ENCODE BETTER

This starts by giving yourself the time that you need in order to learn. Spaced repetition over time is far more effective than one long cramming session (a good analogy is the difference between watering your lawn for ten hours straight on one day, versus for twenty minutes every other day for a month). Research supporting this goes as far back as Hermann Ebbinghaus' "Forgetting Curve" in the 1880s, to Harry Bahrick's research a hundred years later, and many other studies.[134]

The best sort of repetition is what K. Anders Ericsson calls *deliberate practice*, working purposefully and systematically on the things that are most important and challenging.[135] This is the opposite of mindlessly reviewing notes, re-watching lecture recordings, or even practicing a single specific part of the skill you're trying to master (practicing free throws for an hour won't make you much better at basketball). Rather, you focus your attention on the things that are challenging for you to give yourself the best opportunity to learn and improve.

Finally, you must validate whether you really understand something or have just gone over the notes enough times to feel the illusion of fluency.[136] This is done by creating a real-time feedback loop that can let you know whether you're on the right track, and where you need to improve. This can be as involved as an instructor-led process of evaluation and feedback, as complex as using elaborate technology to provide real-time jolts or vibrations in a process of passive haptic learning,[137] or as simple as self-testing using a free flashcard app that uses a process of spaced repetition[138] like Anki. The key is to have a reliable feedback loop that tells you how you're doing.

As much as possible, simulate the environment in which you'll need to remember, ranging from where you study, to *what* you hear, and even *how* you feel. The Tony Marsh Method that Connor Grooms employed to learn Portuguese in a week, for example, involves spending as little time as possible in a classroom, and as much time as possible talking to native speakers. And Canadian astronaut Chris Hadfield recounts in *An Astronaut's Guide to Life on Earth* that the final stages of astronaut training involve running through all their procedures while sitting in the cockpit of the spacecraft. This is done so as to encode the memory as closely as possible to the environment in which it will be retrieved.

If you can't predict exactly how or when you'll need to perform, practice in different contexts and settings, so that the knowledge is encoded more thoroughly in your mind.

These may sound like simple ideas, but they can be powerful and yield spectacular results, as we've seen with examples ranging from remedial education, to rapid language acquisition systems like DuoLingo and Connor Groom's experiments to learn Portuguese in a week. Done correctly, much of the process of learning and remembering knowledge and skill can be cut short. That means you'll have more time left over for the more important work of developing insight.

DID YOU GET ALL THAT?
(LEARNING SELF-ASSESSMENT)

Want to test your understanding of the ideas that we just covered? Or start conversations with interested friends and colleagues? Here are a few questions to guide you:

1. What is the real value in acquiring knowledge?

2. Why is it so hard for humans to remember everything we've ever learned?

3. What is declarative memory?

4. What is procedural memory?

5. What is scaffolding and how does it make learning easier?

6. Even though Edgar Dale's Cone of Experience/Learning sorely lacks factual accuracy, what does it tell us about learning?

7. What does it mean to say that memory is associative?

8. The ability to apply learning is classified as either near transfer or far transfer. How are they different from each other?

9. Spaced repetition over time is an effective way to encode learning, and the best kind of repetition that leads to effective learning is deliberate practice. What does "deliberate practice" mean?

10. Why is a real-time feedback loop important in learning? Give examples.

LIKE WHAT YOU READ, AND WANT TO GO DEEPER?

Here are a few good books to take a look at if you'd like to go deeper on some of the ideas presented in this chapter.

- Benedict Carey's *How We Learn*

- Glenn Whitman & Ian Kelleher's *Neuroteach*

- Brown, Roediger, and McDaniel's *Make It Stick*

- John Hattie and Gregory Yates' *Visible Learning*

- Joshua Foer's *Moonwalking With Einstein*

For more information, including this entire book in digital format plus actionable conversation video guides at the end of each chapter, an expanded and up-to-date bibliography, and additional resources, visit LeveragedLearningBook.com

Insight:
Where Critical Thinking
Meets Creativity

W HEN DILLON HILL was in the fifth grade, his friend Chris was diagnosed with cancer and had to spend months in the hospital. Dillon would visit every day, bringing their favorite video games, because Dillon knew they would make his friend smile. Chris' story ends well: He eventually recovered.

Fast forward to Dillon's senior year in high school. Dillon was volunteering at a food shelter and feeling dissatisfied with the experience. He wanted to see the people whose lives he was impacting, but spent all his time packing bags in the back. "Obviously all these things, they help," Dillon said, "but it just wasn't rewarding." Dillon's mind went back to the video games he had brought to his friend Chris' hospital bed, and that led him to start the charity that eventually came to be called Gamers Gift, bringing virtual reality headsets to children's hospitals, assisted living facilities, and people with disabilities.

"But I mean, we have the Internet, you know? We can figure out anything."

Now, setting up a 501(c) nonprofit isn't simple, and until recently the only way to get it done was to work with a high-priced attorney.

But Dillon filed all the paperwork himself. In his words: "I think we probably Googled every single line on the tax paperwork because we had no idea what a lot of it meant. But I mean, we have the Internet, you know? We can figure out anything."[139]

As inspiring as the actual work and impact of Gamers Gift is, let's focus on the process by which Dillon created it. For a teenager to figure out the legalities of setting up a not-for-profit entity by sheer applying tenacity and a little help from Google is impressive. At the same time, for those who work in specialized fields where much of the work depends on knowledge that most people don't have, it is deeply concerning. The rigorous education required to gain entry to the field of law was once a golden ticket to a secure and prosperous life, and the same is true for other white-collar professions like accounting, banking, engineering, and more. Just completing this challenging and expensive training (and passing the associated professional requirements, like lawyers taking the bar exam) was enough to guarantee a job for those who could make the cut. As the old joke goes, "What do you call the person who graduates at the bottom of his class at medical school? Doctor!"

But Dillon Hill's experience is just one of many points of proof for George Couros' pointed statement in his book *The Innovator's Mindset*: "Information is abundant; it's common."[140] And as anyone with any economics training can tell you (or you can Google for yourself!), the laws of supply and demand dictate that there is a direct trade-off between abundance and value. This is a big problem for many industries, and the most vulnerable sectors may not be the ones you'd expect.

"Information is abundant; it's common."

DISINTERMEDIATION, AUTOMATION, AND THE GREAT HOLLOWING OUT

There was a time when the jobs that were most vulnerable to automation and outsourcing were menial and repetitive. In the early days of technological automation (and indeed, the Industrial Revolution!), there was a lot of low-hanging fruit in the form of jobs that relatively simple technology could automate or accelerate (like bank tellers replaced by ATM machines, receptionists replaced by phone tree systems, and electronic buttons replacing Aldous Huxley's elevator operator), or allow us to ship offshore (like the shipping and communications that make it feasible for so much of what we buy to be manufactured in China).

These days, most of that low-hanging fruit has already been picked, and the fruit on the higher branches is much harder to reach. Further automation of physical work often will take robotics that are much more sophisticated and expensive[141]—so much so that in many cases, it makes sense for businesses to stick with flesh-and-blood employees.

But there's a different kind of low-hanging fruit to be had: the jobs that are less about *doing* and more about *knowing* and relatively rudimentary *thinking* (both tasks that computers are already much better, faster, and more reliable at than we are). The knowing jobs are being eliminated by disintermediation (like real estate or travel agents who are slowly becoming an endangered species now that we can look up listings and itineraries on our own), and the simple thinking jobs are being eliminated by automation through artificial intelligence (like bookkeepers being replaced by QuickBooks and Bench, accountants by TurboTax, and legal researchers by document-reading artificial intelligence).[142] As economist Paul Krugman writes:

> ...The idea that modern technology eliminates only menial jobs, that well-educated workers are clear winners, may dominate popular discussion, but it's actually decades out of date. The fact is that since 1990 or so the U.S. job market has been characterized not by a general rise in the demand for skill, but by 'hollowing out': both high-wage and low-wage employment have grown rapidly, but medium-wage jobs—the kinds of jobs we count on to support a strong middle class—have lagged behind.[143]

THE LEGAL CANARY IN THE HIGHER EDUCATION COAL MINE

This is bad news for professions like law, which is an industry of more than $400 billion per year. Traditional large law firms focus on employing highly trained and high-salaried attorneys, and billing for their work at high rates, even though much of that work involves routine tasks that rarely require expert skill, judgment, or insight.[144] Between services like LegalZoom (where you can set up common legal documents online without consulting a lawyer) and Willing (where you can create a legally binding will for only $69), and the sort of artificial intelligence technology that replaces much legal research, there's a lot less that you need a real lawyer for than you used to. That means less legal work to be done, which means far too few jobs to go around: In 2013, there were more than twice as many law graduates as estimated job openings.[145] This is especially bad news for the law school graduates stuck with an average debt of $125,000. And the students are catching on, as reflected by rapidly declining enrollment numbers (from 100,000 applicants in 2004 to 59,400 in 2013, the lowest number since 1977 and a 33 percent drop from 2010).[146] These are scary numbers, especially now that those in the know consider the legal field to be "the canary in the higher ed coal mine."[147]

Thankfully, there's a silver lining. Although jobs in most of the industry are disappearing, top lawyers are doing just fine and will continue to do so. As British consultant Richard Susskind predicts in his book *The End of Lawyers?*, the future of legal practice is likely to find a cadre of highly paid lawyers at the "center of the doughnut" (to use his metaphor) offering "bespoke services" in complex matters, while the remaining work is farmed out to cheap labor and technology. A similar pattern is likely to emerge with top accountants, doctors, real estate agents, and others because they bring something different to the table than just knowing something that you don't know: They bring insight. As Joseph Aoun expounds:

> Accountants, bankers, attorneys and real estate agents, provide professional services to clients. Other white-collar workers,

such as engineers and architects, provide services to businesses, corporations and government When the economy changes, so must education. It has happened before. We educate people in the subjects that society deems valuable. As such, in the eighteenth century, colonial colleges taught classics, logic, and rhetoric to cadres of future lawyers and clergymen. In the nineteenth century, scientific and agricultural colleges rose to meet the demands of an industrializing world of steam and steel. In the twentieth century, we saw the ascent of professional degrees suited for office work in the corporate economy. Today, the colonial age and the industrial age exist only in history books, and even the office age may be fast receding into memory.

We live in the digital age, and students face a digital future in which robots, software, and machines powered by artificial intelligence perform an increasing share of the work humans do now. Employment will less often involve the routine application of facts, so education should follow suit. To ensure that graduates are 'robot-proof' in the workplace, institutions of higher learning will have to rebalance their curricula. A robot-proof model of higher education is not concerned solely with topping up students' minds with high-octane facts. Rather, it refits their mental engines, calibrating them with a creative mindset and the mental elasticity to invent, discover, or otherwise produce something society deems valuable. This could be anything at all—a scientific proof, a hip-hop recording, a new workout regimen, a web comic, a cure for cancer. Whatever the creation, it must in some manner be original enough to evade the label of 'routine' and hence the threat of automation. Instead of training laborers, a robot-proof education trains creators.[148]

INSIGHT IS NOVELTY ("TELL ME SOMETHING NEW")

Along with Henry Ford, Alfred P. Sloan is one of the founding titans of the American automotive industry. He led General Motors through the Great Depression, German rearmament, fascism, appeasement, and World War II, eventually growing GM into the world's largest corporation. His 1950s memoir, *My Years with General Motors*, is a seminal text in the field of modern management education, and business leaders continue to study the lessons that he taught and the anecdotes that give a glimpse into his management philosophies and ways of thinking. One such anecdote is recounted by brothers Chip and Dan Heath in their book *Decisive*:

> Alfred Sloan, the longtime CEO and chairman of General Motors, once interrupted a committee meeting with a question: 'Gentlemen I take it we are all in complete agreement on this decision here?" All the committee members nodded. "Then," Sloan said, "I propose we postpone further discussion of this matter until our next meeting to give ourselves time to develop disagreement and perhaps gain some understanding of what this decision is about."[149]

Wise leaders through the years have echoed Sloan in their insistence that they prefer employees with the backbone to challenge them and disagree. William Wrigley Jr., who built the chewing gum company that bears his name, famously said, "When two men always agree, one of them is unnecessary."[150] This idea needs constant reinforcement because of the multitude of reasons why voicing disagreement is difficult, especially to people in positions of authority. Challenges range from the fear of real or imagined repercussions, to the simple awkwardness of conflict, and everything in between.

"When two men always agree, one of them is unnecessary."

There's a simple prerequisite to voicing disagreement that doesn't get nearly as much attention: In order to disagree, you need an *insight* that hasn't already been voiced. That insight is a key ingredient to meaningful impact and success, which is the thinking behind investor Peter Thiel's now-famous challenge to entrepreneurs: "Tell me something that's true that nobody agrees with."[151] This is true beyond the realm of Silicon Valley entrepreneurs; across the board, the most successful participants in the modern economy and workplace—whether a leading private equity lawyer, a serial entrepreneur, or an innovative software architect—have in common the ability to provide valuable insight. As our world evolves, having this sort of insight is no longer just the X factor that puts you over the top. Increasingly, it is part of the table stakes for success, as neuropsychologist Elkhonon Goldberg argues in his book *Creativity*:

"Tell me something that's true that nobody agrees with."

> In our time, much of the knowledge acquired in graduate school ten years ago is obsolete today. Most of us don't share an intrinsic interest in science or technology, but even as consumers of technology, we will inhabit a world where tomorrow will be unrecognizably different from today, and our brains will be increasingly challenged by novelty whether we like it or not.[152]

Novelty is the watchword here. Insight necessarily means coming up with something that hasn't already existed: an idea, a connection, or a perspective. Coming up with that sort of novelty, and navigating it effectively, is what it takes to thrive in such a rapidly changing world. But how do we develop insights that are unique, novel, and valuable? Insight isn't just a higher level of knowledge or skill. There's a massive difference between knowing a fact, a procedure, or even a complex process, and being able to provide insight into a challenging, ill-defined problem.

So where do we develop this sort of insight? How do we find what's true that nobody else agrees with? A glaring flaw of most current approaches to education is that they focus entirely on imparting knowledge or fostering proficiency in certain skills. The ability to develop insight is left unexamined. It's often treated as a mysterious, almost magical trait. Sure, we can see and celebrate the outcomes—the insights that lead to new products, solutions, or ways of thinking—but the *capacity* for insight is imagined to be something you either have or lack.

Except that the research and data show that this simply isn't true. Insight lives at the intersection of two rarefied abilities: critical thinking and creativity. Although the current education system does a horrendous job of teaching these things—in fact, strong arguments can be made that conventional education makes you worse at these rather than better—the fact is that we do know what it takes to develop them.

CRITICAL THINKING: SEEING THE OBVIOUS BEFORE IT'S OBVIOUS

Getting stopped at airports is usually a bad thing, but there are exceptions, as American rapper Armando Christian Pérez discovered in 2010. Walking through airports on his way to catch a flight, he would be stopped repeatedly by passers-by wearing T-shirts that said "Zumba." Calling him by his stage name Pitbull, they wanted to tell him that his song *Calle Ocho* ("I Know You Want Me") was one of their favorites. After this happened a few times, Pitbull picked up the phone and called the owners of Zumba Fitness. "You guys are like a radio station," he said, "with DJs in gyms around the world."

Let's pause the story for a moment. What do you imagine the next words out of Pitbull's mouth would be? Certainly, given the modern climate of legitimate concerns of artists and record labels about piracy and copyright infringement, you might expect something along the lines of "You're playing my songs without permission, and you have to pay me." But Pitbull deserves far more credit. When he learned about Zumba playing his song, his mind went to a different problem facing artists: breaking new music to the public.

In the music business, "breaking a new record" refers to the upfront investment that must be made in getting new music enough play time and exposure for audiences to start asking for it. This is critical to the promotion of new music, particularly from lesser-known artists, because research by American psychologist Robert Zajonc has shown that familiarity breeds fondness rather than contempt. Sometimes referred to as the "familiarity principle" or the "mere exposure effect," the basic idea is that the more times we're exposed to a person, idea, or song, the more we tend to like it.[152] That's why a rule of thumb in the music industry is to budget $50,000 for the first three months of marketing a new song.[154]

Unpausing the story, Pitbull continues, "I think you can break records. I'll give you my songs as soon as they launch, and you put them in your Zumba classes." This strategy apparently worked well for Pitbull, whose next album included his first number-one single in the United States. Other musicians took note, and now major artists like Wyclef, Daddy Yankee, Shaggy, and Timbaland work with Zumba to get their songs into one of the thirteen coveted monthly spots that will be played repeatedly to more than fifteen million people each week.[155]

> We make the best decisions we can with the inferences that we draw from the information that we have.

Pitbull's insight illustrates an important realization: We like to believe that we make the best decisions we can with the information that we have, but that isn't true. In fact, we make the best decisions we can *with the inferences that we draw* from the information that we have. The ability to solve complex problems by drawing better inferences and thinking critically is exactly what a 2013 study showed that 93 percent of employers value over an undergraduate degree.[156]

HOW TO DEVELOP CRITICAL THINKING

Let's explore what it takes to develop critical thinking. For that matter, what is critical thinking anyway? The term has become so widely used that it is arguably a bit clichéd. Looking deeper, though, we discover a powerful and nuanced concept. According to the Foundation for Critical Thinking (emphasis added):

Critical thinking is that mode of thinking—about any subject, content, or problem—in which the thinker improves the quality of his or her thinking by skillfully analyzing, assessing, and reconstructing it... thinking that explicitly aims at well-founded judgment and hence utilizes appropriate evaluative standards in the attempt to determine the true worth, merit, or value of something... The critical thinking tradition seeks ways of understanding the mind and then training the intellect so that such 'errors', 'blunders', and 'distortions' of thought are minimized. *It assumes that the capacity of humans for good reasoning can be nurtured and developed by an educational process aimed directly at that end.*[157]

Critical thinking is traditionally taught through repetition and osmosis; if you practice enough and spend enough time in the right environment, those vaunted critical thinking skills will eventually and magically appear. This argument is found most often in the context of the liberal arts—just learn enough different things, and critical thinking skills will automagically appear. But the data show that it doesn't work that way. As Joseph Aoun writes:

In their 2011 study, *Academically Adrift: Limited Learning on College Campuses*, professors Richard Arum and Josipa Roksa found that at least 45 percent of the undergraduates they surveyed showed "exceedingly small or empirically nonexistent" gains in critical thinking, complex reasoning, and written communication during their first two years in college. After four years, 36 percent of their sample still showed no improvement at all: "They might graduate, but they are failing to develop the higher-order cognitive skills that is widely assume college students should master."[158]

Another, ostensibly more directive example is the case method which many business schools have adopted from Harvard Business School. Students review hundreds of case studies of different business scenarios over the course of their degree program. It's an incredibly time-consuming method even when it does work. Unfortunately, for many students, it leads to a kind of brainwashing rather than the restless, independent, critical thinking necessary for deeper insight. Investigative journalist Duff McDonald argues that "[Harvard Business] School is telling [MBA students reviewing cases] what to think, whether they realize that they're doing it or not."[159] He explains:

> Most business schools are adept at the teaching of so-called respondent behavior—solving problems that have already been identified and using facts gathered by someone else. But the sniffing out and exploiting of opportunity is another thing entirely—"operant behavior"—and that's something that can really only be learned by doing.[160]

Clearly we need a better approach to help people develop these skills.

CRITICAL THINKING IN 7 EASY STEPS

We can start by decomposing the broad concept of critical thinking into specific techniques and developing ways to introduce those techniques. For example, the Minerva Schools have developed a new college-level curriculum with a strong focus on seven steps in the process of critical thinking:

1. **Evaluating claims:** One must evaluate the background assumptions as well as the logic that underlies the claim.

2. **Analyzing inferences:** Even if a claim is correct, the inferences one is invited to make from it may not be. Formal logic provides a method for determining which inferences are valid and which are not.

3. **Weighing decisions:** Evaluating claims and analyzing inferences are important in part because they help us decide how to act. To make decisions rationally, one must analyze the various choices and identify their respective trade-offs.

4. **Analyzing problems:** Being able to characterize the nature of the problem.

5. **Facilitating discovery:** There are no recipes or rules for how to make discoveries; however, certain heuristics can set the stage, facilitating discovery. These practices include the ability to create well-formed hypotheses, predictions and interpretations of data.

6. **Solving problems:** One must use creative thinking to solve a problem.

7. **Creating products, processes, and services:** Techniques including iterative design thinking, reverse engineering, and application of the principles of perception and cognition can help to create new products, processes, and services.[161]

Learners who are specifically challenged to evaluate claims, analyze inferences, weigh decisions, and so on, will develop far greater capacity for critical thinking. This, in turn, will make it possible for them to begin developing unique insights in specific situations. Conversely, failure to do so will do nothing more than continue to churn out what former Yale professor William Deresiewicz calls "excellent sheep," which is antithetical to both critical thinking and its sister skill of creativity.

THE CREATIVE MYSTIQUE

In his 2005 Stanford University commencement speech, Apple cofounder Steve Jobs famously told the graduating class and the world about how dropping in on monk Robert Palladino's calligraphy class at Reed College in Oregon was the creative spark that led to beautiful typography on Mac computers.[162] It's a captivating bit of history, with inspiring lessons about following your interests wherever they take you, because you never know when something you learn might end up being useful in the last place you expect.

It isn't a lesson in creativity or how to develop it; if it were that easy, we'd all enroll in calligraphy courses and go on to launch blockbuster electronics products. Alas, creativity isn't so easily developed or even understood. Like critical thinking, the notion of creativity often is seen as mysterious and ineffable. What is the invisible spark that allows artists to create beauty from raw materials, or scientists to discover deep patterns in the structure of the universe, or industrial designers to create products that operate in delightful harmony with our hands?

Creativity is neither just about art, nor limited to geniuses with ground-breaking ideas.

Creativity is neither just about art, nor limited to geniuses with ground-breaking ideas. Creativity is for everyone, and its applications can be as diverse as making things, finding unique solutions, hacking systems, exploiting patterns, curating information, designing systems, leading movements, and creating changes.[163]

COMPONENTS OF CREATIVITY

How do we do it? What are the components of that ever-so-elusive skill of creativity? A great many ingredients collaborate in the creative process, as described by Elkhonon Goldberg in *Creativity*:

- **Salience:** The ability to pose central problems and to ask important questions.

- **Novelty:** An interest in and ability to find solutions for problems not tackled before. It is intellectual nonconformity, the ability to distance oneself from the established scientific theories and concepts, or artistic forms.

- **Ability to relate old knowledge to new problems:** The opposite of novelty, this is the ability to recognize familiar patterns in seemingly new and unique problems.

- **Generativity and mental flexibility:** The ability to generate multiple and diverse approaches to a problem is essential to the creative process in science. A scientist would be exceptionally lucky to hit upon the solution of a daunting problem from the first go.

- **Drive and doggedness:** In a sense, the opposite of the previous, an ability to deploy sustained effort toward tackling a problem. This is about the relationship between inspiration and perspiration.

- **Mental wandering:** The mysterious capacity for the productive and seemingly effortless pursuit of ideas wherever they take you.

- **Mental focus:** The opposite of mental wandering, this is an ability to systemically pursue a logical train of thought.

- **Iconoclastic frame of mind:** In order to forge ahead of society, a creative individual must be driven by a sense of dissatisfaction with the intellectual, scientific, or artistic status quo.

- **Resonance with central societal and cultural themes:** A creative individual, and certainly a genius, is ahead of society, but his/her work must be recognized by society as important and valid in order to survive.

- **Social grace:** Certain supremely creative individuals were known to history for their social suaveness and adaptability, and others for a notorious lack thereof.

- **A favorable cultural milieu:** Historically, certain societies and epochs were richer in discovery and innovation than others. The relationship between a creative individual and his/her social and cultural milieu deserves a closer examination.[164]

Teaching this skill can be a challenge, though, because there's a world of difference between *teaching about* these ideas, and *teaching how* to do actually do it!

TEACHING ABOUT VS. TEACHING TO

Imagine a class for college freshman titled *Introduction to Bicycle Riding*. For week after week, students learn the history, mechanics, and physics of bicycles and bicycle riding. The class is taught by a professor who's never ridden a bike, and an actual bicycle is brought into the classroom only a handful of occasions for students to marvel at but never touch. Finally, graduation day arrives. Students write an exam summarizing their knowledge, and assuming a passing grade, they are taken to the city's busiest highway, given their first bicycle, and told to make their way home.

This sounds absurd until you swap the word *bicycle* out for any number of subjects taught in schools. The more nuanced or situationally-driven a subject is (think entrepreneurship, for example), the more absurdly horrifying it becomes. That difference between *teaching about* a given topic and *teaching to* actually do something—and to the extent that they're taught at all, the skills of creativity and critical thinking that combine to create insight—are at the top of that list.

This is not only regrettable, but also understandable because of how much these skills in particular require a reimagining of the way that we teach. For example, in *The Innovator's Mindset*, George Couros lays out eight elements of a mindset that fits with creative problem-solving and explains how educators can help cultivate this mindset. The approach begins with treating students as partners in the learning process, empowering them to play an active role in their learning, and placing them in environments in which they can explore ideas, work on creative challenges, and learn from one another. This is anathema to the way we've grown up to think of education—from the power dynamics between student and teacher, to the timelines of lessons and assignments and deadlines that leave little room for creative exploration, and everything in between. Much of this is chosen by the student, for the simple reason that the sort of learning we're talking about can be uncomfortable, as Paul Tough explains in *How Children Succeed*:

"It's uncomfortable to focus so intensely on what you're bad at," Brooklyn chess teacher Elizabeth Spiegel told me. "So the way people usually study chess is they read a book about chess, which can be fun and often intellectually amusing, but it doesn't actually translate into skill. If you really want to get better at chess, you have to look at your games and figure out what you're doing wrong."[165]

It's not easy... but we don't have a choice. It's no longer sufficient for education to impart knowledge and skills. Our rapidly evolving economy and culture demand *insight* in addition to knowledge. At first glance, insight can seem like genius, a nearly magical quality that some people have, and some don't. When we probe deeper, though, we discover that insights emerge from critical thinking and creative problem-solving. These capacities can be nurtured through new approaches to learning and growth, but they require creativity and resourcefulness in thinking about what a curriculum should be meant to accomplish and impart, then shifting it dramatically toward the practice of those all-important skills.

HOW TO CULTIVATE CREATIVITY

In the past few decades, researchers have trained their lenses on creativity and discovered that the mystery isn't quite so mysterious. Author Keith Sawyer explains in *Zig Zag*:

> Creativity is not mysterious. Creativity is not a rare insight that comes to you suddenly, once in a lifetime, to change the world. It's just the opposite. Creativity is a way of life. **Creativity is a way of life.** It's a process. The process starts with an idea. But it's not a big insight—it's a small idea. And that small idea can't change the world by itself. In the creative life, you have small ideas every week, every day, even every hour. The key is to learn how to bring those ideas together, over time, and that's the essence of the creative process. The latest creativity research shows the daily practices that exceptional

creators use to keep having those small ideas, and how to bring them together in a creative process that consistently leads to successful creative outcomes.[166]

It's not simple, but it is eminently understandable and if we can *understand* this creative process, then we can help people *learn* it! We don't have to wait for creative insights to pop up magically out of nowhere. We can all train and develop our capacity to work through creative processes, which in turn will yield fresh insights. The process itself is fairly straightforward. Sawyer outlines eight stages:

1. **Ask:** How to ask the right question.

2. **Learn:** Prepare your mind.

3. **Look:** Spot the answers around you.

4. **Play:** Imagine possible worlds.

5. **Think:** How to have great ideas.

6. **Fuse:** How to combine ideas.

7. **Choose:** Make good ideas even better.

8. **Make:** Make your ideas visible.[167]

Clearly we need to do better if we want to foster creative problem solving and help people develop deep insights, starting by incorporating these powerful aspects of creative thinking into different educational experiences. Recent advances in creative education and design thinking make this more feasible than ever before. The most exciting part is that none of the steps in the process is particularly hard. The biggest challenge isn't to follow the steps, but rather to create the time and space for the steps to be followed.

THE IMPORTANCE OF INCUBATION

Even if you mix all the right ingredients in just the right order, you won't have a cake unless you have an oven to put the mixture into, and the time to let it cook. Similarly, all the tools, steps, and frameworks that we've shared in this chapter only work if we bake time into the equation as well. Even the smartest and most creative people can't generate great ideas on command. The "aha!" moment requires that the right stage be set, and that enough time be dedicated to the incubation of the eventual insight.

This isn't a new idea. Way back in 1926, psychologist Graham Wallas conducted a wide-ranging analysis on what poets, scientists, and history's creative thinkers had written about how their insights came to be. Based on that research, he developed a series of mental steps that thinkers take to reach an insight:

- **Preparation.** The initial time spent wrestling with the logical or creative problem in question. This includes not only understanding the specific problem that needs solving and clues or instructions at hand, but also working to the point where all obvious ideas have been exhausted.

- **Incubation.** The stage that begins when you put aside the problem (for example, by abandoning your work and going for a walk in the woods). There are mental processes occurring during this "downtime," and they are crucially important. The mind works on these problems "offline," moving the pieces it has and adding ideas that were held in reserve but not initially considered.

- **Illumination.** The "aha!" moment, when the solution appears seemingly out of nowhere.

- **Verification.** Checking to make sure the resulting insight actually works and holds water.[168]

All four of these steps are crucial, but incubation in particular is likely to be discounted as a frivolous waste of time. It is critical that as both learners and educators, we have the discipline to protect incubation time as the important part of the process that it is. That time creates the shell and context in which creativity can be cultivated, critical thinking can be explored, and insight can finally emerge.

There's just one challenge we haven't tackled yet. Learning and applying these capacities for critical thinking and creativity isn't easy. It takes considerable fortitude to work through the mindset shifts, skill development, and attitude changes necessary to make real progress. In the next chapter, we'll examine this challenge of fortitude and how to address it.

DID YOU GET ALL THAT?
(LEARNING SELF-ASSESSMENT)

Want to test your understanding of the ideas that we just covered? Or start conversations with interested friends and colleagues? Here are a few questions to guide you:

1. What is disintermediation?

2. Give examples of jobs that may soon be eliminated by disintermediation?

3. Menial jobs aren't the only ones getting wiped out. Instead, the U.S. job market has been characterized by a "hollowing out." What does this mean?

4. Top professionals in their fields are doing fine and will continue to do so because they bring something different than just knowing something. What do they bring?

5. Why do wise leaders value and prefer employees who challenge and disagree with them?

6. Insight lives at the intersection of two rarefied talents. What are those talents?

7. What is the "mere exposure effect"?

8. According to a 2013 study, 93 percent of employers value this ability over an undergraduate degree. What is this ability?

9. What is the critical thinking?

10. Critical thinking is traditionally taught through osmosis, repetition, or—as in business schools—the case method. Minerva instead focuses on the seven steps of critical thinking. What are those steps?

11. What are the eight stages of creativity, according to Keith Sawyer?

12. In *The Innovator's Mindset*, George Couros explains an approach for educators to help cultivate a mindset for creative problem solving. What are the three elements of this approach?

LIKE WHAT YOU READ, AND WANT TO GO DEEPER?

Here are a few good books to take a look at if you'd like to go deeper on some of the ideas presented in this chapter.

- George Couros' *The Innovator's Mindset*

- Mihaly Csikszentmihalyi's *Creativity*

- Elkhonon Goldberg's *Creativity*

- Keith Sawyer's *Zig Zag*

For more information, including this entire book in digital format plus actionable conversation video guides at the end of each chapter, an expanded and up-to-date bibliography, and additional resources, visit LeveragedLearningBook.com

And if you'd like to work with my team to develop your own critical thinking skills in a business context, a good place to start is to join one of the free Business Ignition Bootcamps offered by my company Mirasee; details at LeveragedLearning.co/bib

CHAPTER 8

Fortitude:
How the Tough Keep Going
When the Going Gets Tough

Put a spark to a bit of gasoline in a small enclosed space, and the ensuing release of energy can propel a potato five hundred feet. Do the same thing hundreds of times per minute, harness that energy to propel a piston instead of a potato, and you get the propulsive power that can accelerate a Porsche 911 Turbo S to sixty miles per hour in less than three seconds.

This is the technology of internal combustion, which powers every non-electric car on the road today. Whether you ride in a leather-seated luxury vehicle like the aforementioned Porsche or a more modest vehicle sporting children's car seats and a plethora of multi-colored stains creatively engineered by the occupants of those car seats (the story of my life) it's incredible to think that the technology driving your family consists of hundreds of controlled explosions each minute, happening just a few feet away from where you sit.

It's a robust and powerful technology, capable of great things, but it also can be surprisingly delicate. While the "sugar in the gas tank" thing is an urban legend (sugar doesn't actually dissolve in gasoline), there's an even simpler substance that would render an engine inoperable:

water. Because water is heavier than gasoline, all it takes is a few cups of water poured into the fuel tank to float the gasoline and fill the fuel lines with water instead, leaving the engine a sputtering mess.

Our innate ability to learn is a lot like the technological marvel of the internal combustion engine, incredibly powerful and able to propel us great distances. But it also can be very fragile and easily disrupted. That's what happens to far too many students: They get water in their proverbial gas tank, and quit; 28 percent of college students drop out in their first year, and 57 percent aren't done after six years in their so-called four-year program.[169] Technological innovations seem to have made things worse, rather than better, with average MOOC completion rates in the high single or low double digits,[170] and most online courses have drop-out rates as high as 87 percent.[171]

Why does this happen? This is a question that every educator needs to take seriously.

WHY DO SOME PEOPLE QUIT?

As head coach of the Green Bay Packers in the 1960s, Vince Lombardi won more championships than any of his NFL peers. He is famous for his declaration that, "Winners never quit, and quitters never win." Alas, life is sometimes more complex than football. A dogged refusal to quit is the sunk cost fallacy, throwing good money after bad and ignoring the opportunity cost of all the more productive and successful things that you could be doing. In fact, as Seth Godin tells us, winners quit things all the time; "they just quit the right stuff at the right time."[172]

How do you know which is the right thing, and which is the right time? How do you distinguish projects that should rightfully be abandoned from projects undergoing what Godin calls "the dip"—the discouraging and sometimes painful setbacks that are temporary, even if they might not look that way?

Without a crystal ball that can peer into various possible futures, we have to make our best guess, extrapolating from the experiences that we've had and the information that we've collected. This is easier

> Two people can have the same information but draw different inferences. Good inferences lead to good decisions, and bad inferences lead to bad ones.

said than done because as with the challenges of insight, we don't actually make the best decisions we can with the information that we have, but rather with *the inferences that we draw* from the information that we have. Two people can have the same information but draw different inferences. Good inferences lead to good decisions, and bad inferences lead to bad ones.

THE 3 PS OF PESSIMISM

Few people have researched the mental habits that lead to these sorts of inferences and decisions as deeply as Martin Seligman, an authority in the fields of resilience, grit, learned helplessness, optimism, and pessimism. Seligman has identified three patterns of bad inferences that can lead to especially bad decisions, such as quitting a challenge that you would be better off making the effort to complete. He calls them the three Ps of Pessimism: personalization, pervasiveness, and permanence.

1. **Personalization** is the belief that we are at fault for whatever has gone wrong ("it's my fault that this is awful")—like attributing a poor grade to incompetence rather than lack of preparation.

2. **Pervasiveness** is the belief that whatever has gone wrong will affect all areas of life ("my whole life is awful")—like extrapolating a conflict with a co-worker into a belief that nobody likes you.

3. **Permanence** is the belief that the aftershocks will last forever ("and it's always going to be awful")—like believing that losing your job (or quitting school!) will dictate the rest of your life.[173]

The 3 Ps of Pessimism

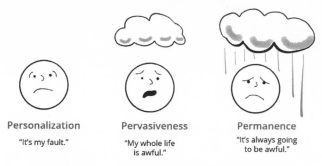

Personalization	Pervasiveness	Permanence
"It's my fault."	"My whole life is awful."	"It's always going to be awful."

Learning is tough, especially if you're trying to learn something that's going to make a discernible impact on your life. You're bound to

> While those challenges and setbacks are objective facts, different inferences can be drawn from them.

run into challenges and setbacks along the way. While those challenges and setbacks are objective facts, different inferences can be drawn from them. If the student is struggling with a particular concept or exercise, for example, rather than inferring that more study and perhaps support are needed, the student per-

sonalizes the failure ("I'm too stupid to learn this"), sees it as pervasive ("I suck at school"), and expects it to be permanent ("I'm never going to be able to do this").

Of course, there's a strong case to be made that these inferences are both mistaken and self-fulfilling. However, if you take them as facts, the decision to quit makes a lot of sense. After all, if it were really true that someone is too stupid to learn a subject, sucks at school, and is never going to be able to do this, why on earth would the student keep investing time, energy, and money in this hopeless endeavor?

You might be tempted to wonder why so many people draw such flawed and damaging inferences from the setbacks that they experience. Perhaps there's a better question that we could ask: Why is it that some people don't?

WHY DO SOME PEOPLE KEEP GOING?

In 1990, Jerry Sternin was sent by Save the Children to fight severe malnutrition in rural Vietnam. Sternin knew well the complex systemic causes of malnutrition, but he considered that knowledge to be TBU—"true but useless"—since changing something as broad and complex as national sanitation, poverty, or education was wholly impractical within the time frame and resources at his disposal.

Instead, he traveled to villages and met with the leading experts on feeding children: village mothers. He asked whether there were any poor families whose children were bigger and healthier than most, and he followed the "yes" answers to discover what the mothers of those children were doing: feeding their children smaller portions of food more often throughout the day, adding brine shrimp to their daily soup or rice dishes, and taking care to ladle from the bottom of the pot, where the shrimp and greens settled. Rather than trying to imagine a solution that doesn't exist, Sternin found a solution that did and trained others to use it, and within six months, 65 percent of the children in the villages where he worked were better nourished.[174]

This approach of looking to replicate what works, rather than solve what doesn't, is called "Finding the Bright Spots" in Chip and Dan Heath's book *Switch*. As Dan explains in *Fast Company*:

> Let's say you launched a new sales process six months ago. So far, the results are mixed. Two reps have doubled their sales. Six are selling about what they were before. Two have slipped. And three are threatening to quit if you don't abandon the idea. What do you do? Well, most managers would put on their problem-solving hats and spend all their time dealing with the three bellyachers. Those two stars can take care of themselves, right? Well, no, you've got it backwards. You should be spending your time trying to clone what those top two are doing. How have they implemented the new process? Maybe they've created some new sales literature, or maybe they've

tweaked the way they approach new leads. If you can get clear on what's working for them, you can spread those answers to your other reps.[175]

Rather than asking why some people quit, the more constructive question to ask, even in situations where continuing forward seems impossible, is why do some people keep on going?

Sooner or later, all students will hit a rough patch. Maybe the subject matter is less interesting or more challenging than they first expected. Maybe they get confused by an assignment or earn a grade that isn't up to their standards. Maybe they're trying to fit this course into an already busy schedule, and they're tired. Maybe there's other life drama going on, fraying their nerves and attention. Even under the best of circumstances, some struggle is unavoidable. As we learned from K. Anders Ericsson, the only way we really learn and get good at something is through deliberate practice, which involves stepping outside your comfort zone and trying activities beyond your current abilities.[176]

Not everyone responds to these challenges in the same way. While some slow down or drop out, others thrive and continue to succeed. What's different about those who succeed, even in the face of stress, trauma, and learning challenges?

BRIGHT SPOTS OF LEARNING

Our first go-to assumption might be that they're smarter, but that isn't it. Gifted students are overrepresented in dropout statistics (statistically speaking they're only about 2.5 percent or 3 percent of the general population,[177] but 4.5 percent of those who drop out of high school).[178] The same is true of discretionary adult education. Thousands of highly intelligent adults drop out of online courses every year. Intelligence alone won't pull you through certain learning challenges.[179]

> Gifted students are overrepresented in dropout statistics.

What's different about those who succeed, it turns out, is that they possess certain non-cognitive capacities: motivation, perseverance, time management skills, work habits, and the ability to ask for feedback and support. These qualities make whatever intelligence we have useful and practical. It's not enough to be brilliant and work on a problem for five minutes, then give up. It's much better to be reasonably smart and keep trying new approaches after your first attempt stalls. If that isn't enough, then go get help from an instructor or a coach, and come prepared with specific questions on how to move forward.

Grade point average in college isn't predicted by intelligence.

Researchers have found that grade point average in college isn't predicted by intelligence as measured by IQ tests or other standardized test scores. Instead, noncognitive academic skills, such as self-control and grit, are key to academic success. These are the skills that fall under the broad umbrella of Positive Psychology, developed by people such as Martin Seligman, who is considered the father of the Positive Psychology movement; his protégé, Angela Duckworth, who wrote the book about grit; Mihaly Csikszentmihalyi, famous for his concept of flow; Carol Dweck, who brought us the Growth Mindset; and many others. As researchers from the University of Chicago Consortium on Chicago School Research explain:

> The prevailing interpretation is that, in addition to measuring students' content knowledge and core academic skills, grades also reflect the degree to which students have demonstrated a range of academic behaviors, attitudes, and strategies that are critical for success in school and in later life, including study skills, attendance, work habits, time management, help-seeking behaviors, metacognitive strategies, and social and academic problem-solving skills that allow students to successfully manage new environments and meet new academic and social demands. To this list of critical success factors, others have added students' attitudes about learning, their beliefs about their own intelligence, their self-control and persistence, and the quality of their relationships with peers and adults.[180]

Or, put more succinctly by economist James Heckman, "Much more than smarts is required for success in life. Motivation, sociability (the ability to work with others), the ability to focus on tasks, self-regulation, self-esteem, time preference, health, and mental health all matter."[181] Let's call this aggregate set of skills fortitude for the sought-after and coveted quality that emerges from them. Fortitude is the hidden key to success, especially in our new world of volitional, online-first learning, where self-motivation and self-regulation are essential.

> The skills of fortitude have a disproportionate impact on our ability to make the most of our good fortunes or transcend the challenges of our bad ones.

I'm not suggesting that that fortitude is the only thing that matters to a person's success, educational or otherwise. There are a multitude of factors, including native intelligence, upbringing, socioeconomic status, and of course luck; and they all have some influence. What I am suggesting—and what the data support—is that the skills of fortitude have a disproportionate impact on our ability to make the most of our good fortunes or transcend the challenges of our bad ones.

HIGH ADVERSITY WITH HIGH SUPPORT

Ideally, the seeds of the crucial noncognitive capacities of fortitude are sown in the formative experiences that we go through as children. The key is not to avoid stress or challenge, but rather to face it with support from those around you. This is the ultimate antidote to the inferences of personalization ("This is difficult stuff. Let's try again."), pervasiveness ("This is hard, but there are many things you've mastered and are doing well."), and persistence ("Some things feel really hard, but eventually and with practice, things get better."). As clinical psychologist Dr. Sherry Walling and her venture capitalist husband, Rob Walling, explain:

> There is certainly a body of literature in the psychological research to support this pattern. High adversity with high

support leads to perseverance, resilience, and grit. As children, these entrepreneurs learned the ability to encounter hard things without folding. They learned to press into their support systems, to find tools to help them move forward, to persevere even in the midst of difficult circumstances.[182]

What if you didn't have that combination of challenges and support as a child? Fortitude is often treated as an unexamined aspect of character: Maybe you can develop it early in life, but past a certain point you either have it or don't. But the data tell a different story, and the most exciting thing about the skills of fortitude is that they are so incredibly malleable. Which is not to say that we aren't best served developing fortitude as children—of course we are. Just as in a perfect world we'd all have good parents, live in stable homes, and be well-provided for. These are important things to aim for as a society, but beyond the scope of what any individual educator can do. As teachers, we can't change someone's intelligence, nor can we change their upbringing or socioeconomic status, but we can teach the component skills of self-discipline, self-regulation, and grit that make up fortitude.

CAN WE LEARN FORTITUDE? THE SCIENCE SAYS YES!

Basketball is a tall person's game. Although there's no technical height minimum for players, there have been only twenty-five players in NBA history with a listed height under 5'10," and only four who were active since 2010.[183] If you stand a modest 5'7" (like me), then it doesn't matter how much you like basketball, you should probably look elsewhere for a successful career path. In the words of legendary entrepreneur and investor Bill Campbell, "You can't coach height."

"You can't coach height."

By the same token, Nobel laureates need to be on the top extreme of the intelligence curve, Seal Team Six requires the best in physical fitness, and the highest political offices require remarkable charisma and ability to influence. When we think about elite performers, we tend to focus on these essential traits of the remarkable few who make the headlines. Yet this attention to world-class performers leads us astray when it comes to education and learning, because it focuses too heavily on traits and not enough on skill. World-class performance requires a combination of both; the *trait* of height (and coordination) combined with the *skill* developed by ten thousand hours of focused, deliberate practice.

We all can learn and grow by focusing on our noncognitive capacities of motivation, perseverance, time management skills, work habits, and the ability to ask for feedback and support.

The research that has shown us how malleable the various components of fortitude can be to interventions is proof that, contrary to what many believe, fortitude is not a trait, or a virtue, as Aristotle called it so long ago. It is a skill, and skills can be developed. Although most of us will never play in the NBA, we all can significantly improve our fitness, health, and enjoyment of sports, and to do that, we must focus on the environment in which we learn about physical activity, the mindset we adopt, and the lifelong habits we're forming. By the same token, we all can learn and grow by focusing on our noncognitive capacities of motivation, perseverance, time management skills, work habits, and the ability to ask for feedback and support.

Fortitude is not only something that can be taught, but also something that modern educators must teach. These are the critical skills of success in the modern world, and without them, many of our students can't even complete the training that we currently provide. It is incumbent on all educators to provide whatever fortitude training is necessary for their students to complete their learning and reap the promised results.

The prospect of supporting people to develop these crucial skills is exciting, but how do we do it? We can hope that people stumble into circumstances that provide high adversity with high support, or we can carefully engineer these circumstances for our learners and provide the tools to make them successful.

HOW CAN WE DEVELOP FORTITUDE?

We can lean on a good deal of research that has been done into what key skills are most important for educators to impart. In their book *Neuroteach*, Glenn Whitman and Ian Kelleher lay out the key noncognitive factors that have been linked to learning success, as well as the key mindsets that contribute to academic performance. The noncognitive factors are academic behaviors (attending class, being engaged, participating, and completing assignments); academic perseverance (grit, tenacity, self-control, and delayed gratification); social skills (cooperation, assertion, responsibility, and empathy); and learning strategies (study skills, metacognition, self-regulation, and goal-setting). The four key mindsets are a sense of belonging ("I belong in this learning community"); implicit theories of ability ("my ability and competence grow with my effort," also known as the Growth Mindset); self-efficacy ("I can succeed at this"); and expectancy-value theory ("this work has value for me").[184]

Whitman & Kelleher's Concepts

Non-Cognitive Factors to Learning Success

1. Academic behaviors (attending class, being engaged, participating, and completing assignments)

2. Academic perseverance (grit, tenacity, self-control, and delayed gratification)

3. Social skills (cooperation, assertion, responsibility, and empathy)

4. Learning strategies (study skills, metacognition, self-regulation, and goal-setting)

4 Key Mindsets for Successful Learning

1. Sense of belonging - "I belong in this learning community"

2. Implicit theories of ability (also known as the Growth Mindset) - "my ability and competence grow with my effort"

3. Self-efficacy - "I can succeed at this"

4. Expectancy-value theory - "this work has value for me"

It is admittedly a long list, but as educators, we can work with this. Essentially, there are four things that our students need us to do in order to support them in developing fortitude:

1. **Support successful behaviors**. Foster engagement; be creative in encouraging participants to attend live classes and participate in online discussions; provide incentives and support for completing assignments.

2. **Provide scaffolding for perseverance**. It's not enough to just tell students, "You need to keep trying!" We must seek to develop creative ways to help students understand the kind of challenges they will face, and to persist through those challenges even when it doesn't feel immediately rewarding for them.

3. **Create opportunities for cooperation and taking initiative**. Education feels most difficult when one has the sense of being isolated and alone in a course. When there are opportunities to cooperate with others, take initiative to help others, and become part of a tribe (even a virtual one). Learning becomes more meaningful and more fun. As a side benefit, participants can sharpen their social skills along the way.

4. **Help learners understand and develop their own learning strategies**. It's possible to become an expert in the process of learning itself. The best students do so well in part because they have mastered their own learning strategies. They are self-aware about when they understand a concept and are able to take action on it. They set personal goals and track their progress toward those goals. For others who haven't mastered these approaches on their own, we can help coach them toward more effective learning.

An important key here is to figure out how to share those tools so that people not only understand them, but also adopt and use them. This is the teaching about vs. teaching to challenge again. The best tools won't do any good if students learn about them but fail to make any changes in their behavior. The good news is that we aren't flying blind here. There's a massive research base from the fields of positive psychology and neuroscience to draw upon. We can cherry-pick the best research-proven techniques, try them with our own students, and tweak them over time.

The good news comes with the important caveat that these non-cognitive capacities are highly individual, which means that the way you help others develop these capacities will depend on both your unique style and theirs. A hard-charging fitness coach approach of "tough love, no excuses!" may instill persistence with its in-your-face challenges, but that won't work with every student. By the same token, an intuitive and energetic approach of spiritual healing may support positive growth, but again, it won't work with every student. We must lean on our strengths and at the same time be adaptive and malleable to our students' needs.

So now let's get more actionable, and break out four specific approaches to developing these sorts of skills. Each is backed by research, and each is something you can integrate in direct, practical ways.

START WITH MOTIVATION

It all begins with motivation. If learners aren't motivated, there's no tool or hack that can make a difference for them. They'll just give up when the going gets tough. As we've seen, though, not everyone gives up. Some people keep on going, most especially those possesses of Angela Duckworth's quality of grit. But as Caroline Adams Miller explains, there's no such thing as being "gritty" about everything. Grit is specific to the things that we care about.[185] But where does that grit come from? Where do we find that motivation to keep on going, even though the going is tough?

Research into self-determination theory has demonstrated the importance of having intrinsic motivation: doing something because it is interesting and enjoyable, or at least an expression of one's values and identity, rather than doing it because one feels compelled by external forces. Intrinsically motivated people try harder and longer, perform more flexibly and creatively, and learn more deeply than extrinsically motivated people.[186]

What may come as a surprise is that intrinsic motivation can be undermined by extrinsic demands, such as rewards, prizes, grades, and social pressures. In a traditional academic setting, this means that incentive systems such as grades and rewards can lead students to lose sight of their own intrinsic motivations.[187] When this happens, they can begin working only for the extrinsic rewards, and the benefits of intrinsic motivation (persistence, flexibility, creativity, and deep learning) fade away.

HELP LEARNERS DEVELOP SELF-DISCIPLINE

The second approach is to help learners develop self-discipline, but not in the way you might think. Discipline is often confused with self-denial, such as undertaking an unpleasant cleanse diet or forcing yourself to work harder and longer. In fact, discipline is about the presence of mind to choose what you actually want over what you might feel like in the moment. The path to making self-disciplined choices is through practices of mindfulness and gratitude, which open us up to more and larger perspectives.

Mindfulness has become an incredibly hot topic in recent years, so you've probably heard that mindfulness practices have been demonstrated to decrease depression, anxiety, and diverse stress-related disorders. More important for education, mindfulness can increase self-efficacy, which is a key contributor to learning. But exactly what is mindfulness?

Mindfulness is often described as a type of awareness: a way of relating to all experience—positive, negative, and neutral—in an open and receptive way. This awareness involves freedom from grasping and from wanting anything to be different. It simply knows and accepts what is here, right now. This mindfulness involves knowing what is arising as it arises, without adding anything to it, trying to get more of what we want (pleasure, security), or pushing away what we do not want (fear, shame).

Psychologists Shauna Shapiro and Linda Carlson have developed a model of mindfulness comprising three core elements: intention, attention, and attitude. Intention refers to knowing why we are practicing mindfulness, and understanding our personal vision and motivation. Attention involves observing the operations of one's moment-to-moment, internal and external experience. And attitude refers to the qualities one brings to attention, and includes a general sense of openness, acceptance, curiosity, and kindness.[188]

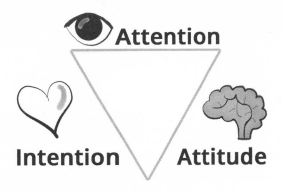

A mindful learner is able to relate openly and flexibly to the diversity of experiences that come with learning new skills—taking in stride whatever problems, challenges, or feelings of "stuckness" arise. When faced with distractions, they think clearly about what really matters and what must be set aside.

TEACH MENTAL CONTRASTING

Once learners are focused and moving forward, they'll learn enough to start taking on more difficult challenges, which will lead to setbacks and temporary failures. Specific strategies can begin to help them cope with the up-and-down nature of learning progress. One powerful strategy is called *mental contrasting*, essentially preparing people for challenges before they occur.

This concept comes from Gabriele Oettingen, a leading psychologist at New York University. She explains in her book *Rethinking Positive Thinking* that both optimists and pessimists have consistent flaws in their thinking, which lead to subpar performance when faced with setbacks. Optimists are all about "indulging." They fantasize about the amazing future they are going to have and how good they'll feel when they learn everything in their course. This feels great at the time, but doesn't lead to achievement, because everything comes crashing down after the first significant problem crops up.

Pessimists instead get stuck in "dwelling." They think about all the barriers to their learning and why they won't be able to achieve their goals. For example, a pessimist in a watercolor class might dwell on how her paintings never turn out the way she hopes, how she doesn't have anything interesting in her yard to paint, and so on. You probably won't be shocked to learn that pessimistic dwelling doesn't lead to successful learning, either.

Mental contrasting is a clever alternative to both types of flawed thinking. The trick is to concentrate on a positive outcome and simultaneously to imagine potential obstacles on the path to success. Oettingen teaches the easy-to-remember mnemonic WOOP for the steps in doing this:

1. **Wish.** What is an important wish that you want to accomplish? Your wish should be challenging but feasible.

2. **Outcome.** What's the result you envision? Really pause and take a little time to visualize the desired outcome.

3. **Obstacle.** What's the main obstacle that might prevent you from achieving that outcome?

4. **Plan.** What's an effective action to overcome that obstacle? Make a "when-then" plan; WHEN you encounter that obstacle, THEN you'll take this action.[189]

Gabriele Oettingen's WOOP Method

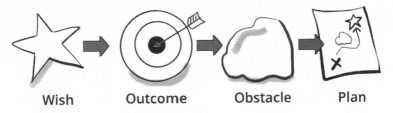

Wish   Outcome   Obstacle   Plan

1. **Wish: What is an important wish you want to accomplish?**

_____

2. **Outcome: What's the result you envision?**
   (Pause and visualize the desired outcome.)

_____

3. **Obstacle: What's the main obstacle that might prevent you from achieving that outcome?**

_____

4. **Plan: What's an effective action to overcome that obstacle?**
   (Make a "when-then" plan: WHEN you encounter that obstacle, THEN you'll take this action.)

_____

CULTIVATE A GROWTH MINDSET

Struggle, challenge, and difficulty are enormously beneficial for learning, long-term memory, and skill development, even though intuitively, we feel as if we're failing and falling behind. It feels great to absorb a new idea presented in an interesting way or to "check the box" of completing a relatively easy task. However, it feels deeply uncomfortable to work on a project and not achieve the desired outcome, or to submit an assignment and receive critical feedback.

The best teachers find ways to support people through this uncomfortable curve of growth. Specifically, according to Whitman and Kelleher, teachers should help students develop an iterative process of trying strategies, evaluating progress, and then refining or finding new ones. We should coach our learners to deal positively with failure, seek out challenges, and value mastery goals rather than performance goals.

Each of the previous strategies contributes here as well. Motivation is essential; self-discipline enables taking thoughtful and constructive action after a setback; and mental contrasting puts plans in place to deal with challenges before they occur.

To go further, we can combine these strategies with encouraging our learners to develop a growth mindset. Around ninth grade, most people begin to shift from a *growth mindset* to a *fixed mindset*. This means they begin to think of their intelligence and other abilities as fixed traits that they are born with and must accept. They become increasingly afraid to take intellectual risks or make mistakes for fear of hurting their grades.

A fixed mindset is anathema to learning and development. The most successful students aren't afraid to take risks or fail when learning. They trust in themselves to learn from each mistake and get better in the process. One of the most effective things we can do for all our students is to help them adopt this constructive, creative mindset.

So now we've explored the three components of Leveraged Learning: knowledge, insight, and fortitude. We've dug into each of them in turn, and what it takes to build them into a learning experience that leads to the success that all educators owe to their students. Now let's turn our attention to the last piece of the puzzle, which is the process of building actual learning experiences.

DID YOU GET ALL THAT?
(LEARNING SELF-ASSESSMENT)

Want to test your understanding of the ideas that we just covered? Or start conversations with interested friends and colleagues? Here are a few questions to guide you:

1. What are the 3 Ps of Pessimism?

2. Even gifted students and intelligent adults drop out of school. What's different about those who do succeed?

3. What are the skills that make up fortitude?

4. According to the book, *Neuroteach*, what are the key non-cognitive factors that have been linked to learning success?

5. What are the four key mindsets that contribute to academic performance?

6. What four things do students need educators to do for them?

7. What research-backed approaches can educators apply to help people learn and develop?

8. What kind of motivation is the right kind for learning—intrinsic or extrinsic motivation? Why?

9. How can external rewards undermine intrinsic motivation and, ultimately, learning?

10. If self-discipline is not self-denial, then what is it?

11. What practices help people make self-disciplined choices?

12. According to Shapiro and Carlson, what are the three core elements of mindfulness?

13. What is mental contrasting?

14. Describe the steps in Gabriele Oettingen's WOOP method.

15. What is a growth mindset as opposed to a fixed mindset? Which one is better for learning?

LIKE WHAT YOU READ, AND WANT TO GO DEEPER?

Here are a few good books to take a look at if you'd like to go deeper on some of the ideas presented in this chapter.

- Martin Seligman's *Flourish*

- Angela Duckworth's *Grit*

- Carol Dweck's *Mindset*

- Paul Tough's *How Children Succeed*

For more information, including this entire book in digital format plus actionable conversation video guides at the end of each chapter, an expanded and up-to-date bibliography, and additional resources, visit LeveragedLearningBook.com

CHAPTER 9

Designing Great Courses

CONTRARY TO what you may have heard, Albert Einstein was a brilliant student since early childhood. He couldn't stand authoritarian teachers, though, so much so that when he was five years old, he threw a chair at his tutor because he couldn't stand his style.[190] This led his teacher to proclaim that "he would never amount to much." Albert's mother, Pauline Einstein, would have none of that. She went out and bought several books then started teaching Albert by herself.[191] Here we see the tripartite foundation of success: the knowledge that Einstein easily assimilated from his classes and his mother's textbooks; the insight of curiosity and critical thinking that is instinctive to all children and that he refused to let a teacher drum out of him; and the fortitude of facing adversity with the love and support of his mother.

That foundation, combined with Einstein's natural talent and a healthy dose of serendipity, led to one of the most impressive academic careers in history, with peaks including proposing his theory of general relativity, winning the Nobel Prize in Physics in 1921, and devising the most recognized formula in the world, $E=mc^2$. We should take special note when Einstein tells us, "Imagination is more important than knowledge. For knowledge is limited, whereas imagination embraces the entire world, stimulating progress, giving birth to evolution."

"Imagination is more important than knowledge."

Einstein was not only a smart man, but also a wise man. He understood that there are two kinds of problems in the world: the ones where there's a right answer and the ones where there isn't. In the realms of physics, math, or biology, things work the way that they work, and it's on us to figure out which way that is. That's why the laws of physics are discovered rather than invented. They continue to exist whether we discover them or not. Some of these problems are incredibly hard, but they nonetheless have right answers waiting for us to find. However, in the realm of art, literature, and music, there is no right answer to be discovered. Instead, there are many possible answers for us to imagine and create.

The challenge of education is that doing it well is both kinds of challenge. There's a science to effective instruction and empowerment, as we've explored. There's also an art to an effective explanation, compelling metaphor, and engaging delivery adding up to more transformation than the sum of their individual parts would suggest. Let's learn from the sort of people who deal with these part-science and part-art challenges every day.

HOW TO L.A.U.N.C.H. A COURSE

If anyone can be called an expert on solving problems that don't have right answers, it's David Kelley, founder of the iconic design firm IDEO. Kelley's design teams routinely are enlisted to design things ranging from the perfect shopping cart[192] to a better cubicle.[193] But they aren't experts in shopping carts, cubicles, or any of the other products that they design. How do they do it?

IDEO's secret weapon, which is shared by the entire design industry, is the process called design thinking. Educators John Spencer and A.J. Juliani explain this process, using the acronym LAUNCH:

- **Look, listen, learn.** Before you can set about solving a problem, developing an idea, or addressing an issue or a need, you must understand it and the people affected by it. This is done by cultivating curiosity about and empathy for your students and their learning objectives.

- **Ask lots of questions.** Take the time to explore the issue and problem in detail. Not the solution, mind you, just the problem. Ask students what they find interesting or challenging, and ask experts what is surprising or effective.

- **Understand the problem or process.** This is where your questions and discussions are supplemented with research into industry knowledge and best practices. With clarity on the true problem to be solved, we can draw from the best there is by way of solutions.

- **Navigate ideas.** This is where you start brainstorming solutions, leveraging some of the lessons on creativity shared in earlier chapters. Then you evaluate ideas on their merits, and brainstorm some more to see what emerges that is worth developing into a solution.

- **Create.** Finally, you're ready to turn ideas into something real, by building a prototype, making a model, or writing a draft. In the world of course building, we call this first run at your course and curriculum a "pilot," which will tend to be rough around the edges, but good enough.

- **Highlight what's working and failing.** Monitor the successes and challenges as you go to find glitches and friction points, and see what needs to be revised, what needs to be reinforced, and what needs to be scrapped completely and replaced. This comes back to the start of the cycle.[194]

This process is robust, powerful, and effective for the simple reason that it adopts a stance of learning, iterating, and improving over just building and delivering. Only one of the six steps in the LAUNCH process is the direct development and presentation of a curriculum. You're always learning and never quite done.

THE BETA MENTALITY

How do you measure or quantify an artist's success? Is it in the fame or notoriety? The quality of the work? The impact on other artists? Or how sought after the artist's work is hundreds of years after he or she is gone? By all these measures, Leonardo da Vinci was a huge success, but by others, much less so. Leonardo's multifaceted mind constantly jumped between fields of study and projects of interest, and he was notorious not only for the quality of his works, but also for the incredible length of time it took him to finish them... if he finished them at all. This is best illustrated with the *Mona Lisa*, which is considered his greatest masterpiece. He worked on the *Mona Lisa* for the last 17 years of his life, and it never was delivered to the patron who commissioned it.

This might be fine if Leonardo himself was happy with the outcomes, but history suggests otherwise. Yes, his surviving work is among the most valuable in the world—for example, the recently discovered and restored *Salvator Mundi* painting, which most scholars attribute to Leonardo, was sold for an unprecedented $450 million, the most anyone in the world has ever paid for a painting.[195] But Leonardo himself never saw any of that money. Throughout his career, he was dependent on the patronage of aristocrats and leaders who were willing to indulge his eccentricities. Contrast that with his contemporary and rival Michelangelo, who sculpted *David* and painted the Sistine Chapel; when he died, he left an estate of 50,000 florins,[196] which translates to more than $40 million in today's money.

What was the key to Michelangelo's success? At least part of it was that he buckled down, did the work, and delivered to his patrons—over two hundred pieces of art, compared with only a few dozen pieces by Leonardo da Vinci. In short, Steve Jobs got it right: Real artists ship!

Steve Jobs got it right: Real artists ship!

And shipping means compromise. Even Jobs, who was a notorious perfectionist (which led to numerous production and product release delays), could ship only the best product that could be made with the technology of the time. For a perfectionist to make that sort of compromise takes a quality not often associated with Jobs: humility, which is the root of what Jeff Cobb calls the Beta Mentality,[197] which is the ability to overcome the idea that the perfect product must be produced right out of the gate. But at the same time, if shipping means compromise, then that means any course we produce won't be as good as it ultimately could be, and it becomes incumbent on us as course creators to go back and fix it.

MOMENTUM TOWARD LEARNING AND SUCCESS

An idea shared at a dinner party morphs into an article, which garners enough interest to indicate that you've got something, so you get to work writing a book. Weeks stretch to months and even years, as you pore through research, talk to experts, and write drafts of chapters. The process is long and solitary, and it comes at a cost of time that could be spent playing with your children, talking to your spouse, or even doing something that makes a few dollars. But you believe in what you're doing, so you persist through the circuitous journey of ideas that are half-developed, metaphors that worked in your head but don't on paper, and chapter drafts that are scrapped upon realization that the book needs to go in a different direction. Finally, one day, you emerge from your writer's cave with a completed manuscript.

You're tempted to celebrate. After all, you've worked so hard, and feel like you've come so far. But this is just the beginning. Now it's time to share that precious manuscript with the smartest people you know and brace yourself for their unvarnished feedback. And boy, does that feedback come. You quickly learn that your spelling isn't nearly as precise as you thought, you use semi-colons more often than anyone should, and what you proudly called eloquence was really long-windedness. Having addressed style, your well-meaning reviewers take on the work itself. While they're careful to remind you that they see potential, your thinking is muddled, your metaphors are unclear, and the conceptual framework you are building is far weaker in places than you care to admit. The critique experience is dizzying, and absurd amounts of energy are dedicated to single sentences, as you struggle to separate opinions that you legitimately disagree with from truths that you simply don't want to hear. It isn't easy, but it is necessary and worthwhile. Ultimately, a book is only as good as the difference that it makes in the minds and lives of those who read it.

The same is true of a course. We find a problem that can be solved by education, and we think through the knowledge and skills that we want to teach, the insight that we want to cultivate, and the fortitude that we want to impart. Then we navigate the LAUNCH cycle and work through the six layers of Leveraged Learning to craft our course. Finally it's time to work with our first cohort of students, and invariably we learn that our explanations aren't as clear as we thought, and our students aren't nearly as motivated as we expected. That's not to mention that our technology is hard, our accountability is proving ineffective, and the success behaviors that we painstakingly designed don't seem to be taking hold. Thankfully, we overcompensated with support for our students, and with what feels like Herculean effort, we got them over the finish line.

Am I dramatizing a little? In some cases yes, and in some cases not at all. What is absolutely true, though, is that creating a course is just the beginning of a much longer journey. Every educator needs real world feedback as to what is working, and what isn't, so much so that Bill Gates took the TED stage in 2013 to propose that the best investment of $5 billion the United States could make would be in building extensive systems to provide feedback to teachers.[198] For that feedback to be effective, it will focus on two factors: momentum, and friction.

PROGRESS: MOMENTUM VS. FRICTION

Newton's first law of motion states that an object will remain in motion unless acted upon by an external force. In space, that means a little push is all it takes to get you clear across the galaxy, as long as you have enough time and don't bump into anything along the way.

Down here on Earth, though, there are lots of external forces such as air pressure, gravity, and friction. As a result, no matter how hard you throw a ball, it will go only so far before slowing and crashing.

Learners' journey through any educational experience works in much the same way. They set out with a certain amount of momentum, and that momentum gradually is decayed by friction and distraction. If the friction or distraction become greater than the momentum forward, they stop dead in their tracks. Game over. As educators, our jobs are to plot the course from start to finish (meaning the transformation that comes from the successful application of whatever we're teaching) and find where along the way friction is breaking momentum. With that clarified, we can eliminate friction, add momentum, or do both, to keep students moving forward. Which begs the question: What creates friction?

WHAT CREATES FRICTION?

Far too many attics and garages are littered with the remnants of unmet goals: the guitar that we never learned to play, the exercise machines that didn't get us in shape, the skis that rode the slopes only three times, the running shoes that never turned into a running habit, and the tools that never made household repairs. Why do we fail to achieve so much of what we set out to achieve? The answer is that in all cases, the challenge is one of changing behavior, and changing behavior is hard. Jonathan Haidt, in his book *The Happiness Hypothesis*, lays out a model for thinking about the three areas in which we can face friction in pursuit of our goal, with the metaphor of a rider on an elephant navigating a path:

- **The rider** loves to contemplate and analyze, doing so with a negative bias, almost always focusing on problems rather than solutions. The rider is frustrated by uncertainty and easily exhausted. The rider is your rational mind, typified by the prefrontal cortex that looks for patterns, makes plans, predicts the future, monitors the self, and attempts to distinguish between and suppress animal instincts.

- **The elephant** is easily spooked and hates doing things with no immediate benefit. It is stubborn, needs reassurance, and is quickly demoralized. It is powerful, tireless, and difficult to actively direct. The elephant is your emotional mind, typified by the amygdala that is the root of fear and trigger of the body's stress response. Negative emotion has a narrowing effect on range of thought, while positive emotion allows the mind to wander creatively.

- **The path.** Even when the rider and the elephant cooperate, they must know what direction to head. Without a clear vision of the destination, change will not happen, as the elephant tends to follow the path of least resistance. The path is the environment, the external stimuli making up the world that the mind consciously and unconsciously interprets and reacts to. Forces such as convenience, distraction, and cognitive biases play a significant role in directing behavior.[199]

Rider = Rationality
Elephant = Emotions
Path = Environment

HOW TO REMOVE FRICTION

Through the lens of this model, we can see that friction comes in three forms, which tech entrepreneur, Sachin Rekhi, in his article titled, "The Hierarchy of User Friction," calls interaction friction (path problems), cognitive friction (rider problems), and emotional friction (elephant problems).[200] Note that the change in order (first from rider to elephant to path then from path to rider to elephant) is intentional. The first order helps to understand the metaphor, and the second order is the way you look to solve problems. Let's explore each in turn:

- **Solving interaction friction, aka path problems.** We live in an age of technological marvel, where everything we want is a key press or voice command away. To say that this has made us impatient is an enormous understatement, so much so that Amazon's tests show that a page speed slowdown of just one second could cost $1.6 billion in sales each year.[201] As a course creator who slaves over a lesson only to find that students abandon it because of the smallest technical challenge, this can be frustrating, but it's also good news. In the grand scheme of things, fixing user experience challenges is fairly simple. The first step is to audit the students' experience and get a sense of any steps that might create more friction than necessary. If you find them, fix them. As Rekhi writes, "We strive to build intuitive and consistent interfaces to prevent interaction friction. We ensure our call-to-actions are prominent, we reduce the number of steps or fields in our forms, we leverage style guide lines to ensure we have a consistent UX across all of our experiences, and we try to do the work for the user so they don't have to whenever we can. These are just a few of the techniques that are commonly used to address interaction friction."[202]

- **Solving cognitive friction, aka rider problems.** This is about cognitive load, as Rekhi explains: "Cognitive load refers to the total amount of mental effort being used in working memory. When cognitive load is high when performing a task, it means there is significant cognitive friction. The designer's goal then becomes minimizing cognitive friction. Cognitive friction is broader than just interaction friction as it encompasses all aspects of the experience that result in mental effort." In other words, if something is confusing your students—whether it's your instructions or your actual lessons—that can create cognitive friction that the students can't handle. Again we audit the experience, looking for the questions that keep recurring, the dropoffs in student engagement, or the work that often comes back wrong, all of which point to confusion. And again, if you find it, fix it.

- **Solving emotional friction, aka elephant problems.** We turn to this last because it's the hardest sort of friction to solve, often requiring that we empower our students with hard-won fortitude. In other words, easier said than done. This is about the stuff that we know how to do and have a clear path to accomplish, but that we don't feel comfortable doing. For example, explaining the mechanics of how to sell is fairly straightforward, and students can memorize a script without much difficulty. But actually navigating a sales conversation and addressing questions of value and affordability is uncomfortable because money can be uncomfortable.

So we audit our course over and over again, looking for any friction that we can eliminate or reduce. Just as a book can and should undergo multiple rounds of revision, most courses must undergo multiple rounds of iteration. You develop the course, present it to students, and measure the results. This leads to learning about what worked and what didn't, plus hypotheses about how you might do better. That in turn leads to a new iteration, new feedback, and new learning, in a cycle that keeps on going.

The Lean Start-Up Cycle

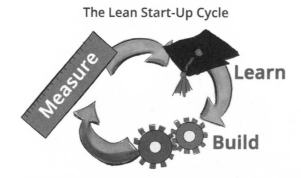

Student results improve over time, and you start seeing diminishing returns on new iterations and improvements. Your course is now robust. At long last, you've built something stable and truly transformative. Now, at a macro level, we've covered the entire process, but when it comes to creating a good course and iterating it into a great one, there are many layers of nuance that go into getting it just right. We'll explore those layers in the next, and final, chapter.

DID YOU GET ALL THAT?
(LEARNING SELF-ASSESSMENT)

Want to test your understanding of the ideas that we just covered? Or start conversations with interested friends and colleagues? Here are a few questions to guide you:

1. What are the elements of the tripartite foundation of success?

2. The design firm, IDEO, uses a six-step process called "design thinking," and it has the acronym, LAUNCH. What does LAUNCH stand for?

3. What is the meaning of a "beta mentality"?

4. In what way is a course similar to a book?

5. What two factors decay a learner's momentum?

6. Even with the best of intentions, learners can lose momentum and fail to complete a course. What is the educator's job so their students keep moving forward?

7. In Jonathan Haidt's metaphor for behavior change, what do the rider, the elephant, and the path represent?

8. What are the three forms of friction, according to Sachin Rekhi?

9. Give examples of how a course creator can remove or reduce Interaction Friction (aka Path Problems).

10. What is the meaning of "cognitive load"?

11. What are some indicators that your students are finding something confusing?

12. Which kind of friction is hardest to solve?

13. How can teachers use the Lean Startup Cycle to create better courses?

LIKE WHAT YOU READ, AND WANT TO GO DEEPER?

Here are a few good books to take a look at if you'd like to go deeper on some of the ideas presented in this chapter.

- Jeff Cobb's *Leading the Learning Revolution*

- A.J. Juliani and John Spencer's *Empower*

- My own book, *Teach and Grow Rich*

For more information, including this entire book in digital format plus actionable conversation video guides at the end of each chapter, an expanded and up-to-date bibliography, and additional resources, visit LeveragedLearningBook.com

And if you'd like to put out your own shingle as an educator entrepreneur, a good place to start is to join one of the free Course Building Bootcamps offered by my company Mirasee; details at LeveragedLearning.co/cbb

The Six Layers of Leveraged Learning

G GREAT CHEFS know that all dishes and flavors are created by some blend of the presence or absence of five basic tastes: sweet, sour, bitter, salty, and umami (savory). In much the same way, every learning experience is the product of six different components, each layered on top of the next: content, success behaviors, delivery, user experience, accountability, and support. Let's explore each of them in turn.

#1 CONTENT: WHAT WILL BE TAUGHT TO GET STUDENTS WHERE THEY'RE GOING

The base layer of Leveraged Learning is the actual content of delivery, hence the emphasis of the Spencer and Juliani's LAUNCH cycle on taking the time to get it right, which is informed by deeply understanding the problem and by having our sights clearly set on the goals we seek to achieve.

Michael Palmer, an associate professor and associate director of the University of Virginia's Teaching Resource Center, created a program called the Course Design Institute to help professors better design their courses. This foundational exercise of their "backward-integrated design" approach to course planning is recounted in Chip and Dan Heath's book *The Power of Moments:*

> On the afternoon of the first day of the Course Design Institute, Palmer introduces an activity called the 'Dream Exercise,' inspired by an idea in L. Dee Fink's book *Creating Significant Learning Experiences.* He puts the following question to his audience of twenty-five to thirty professors: "Imagine that you have a group of dream students. They are engaged, they are perfectly behaved, and they have perfect memories. ... Fill in this sentence: 3-5 years from now, my students still know. Or they still are able to do. Or they still find value in."[203]

We must begin with the end in mind.

With a nod to the late Stephen R. Covey, we must begin with the end in mind, with a clear picture of what we want our students to know, feel, and do. That is the first of three steps, as laid out by Marjorie Vai and Kristen Sosulski:

1. **Begin with the learning outcomes.** Check that the learning outcomes are the ones that are important and meaningful to the student.

2. **Work backward and plan out the assessments.** In other words, how will we know (i.e. measure) whether our students have achieved the outcomes or not?

3. **Work backward again, to use the assessments as the measure of the content.** In order to achieve these goals, what do students need to know? And how well do they need to know it? In order for us to impart that level of knowledge and skill, what do we need to communicate and share?

4. **Work backwards a third time, to the scaffolding they'll need in order to understand.** What knowledge and experience will make the training comprehensible and accessible to the learner.

What is the background that you as the instructor take for granted, that might be beyond the student's grasp. Most importantly, what can you do to bridge that gap for them?

5. **Prune your curriculum mercilessly.** This is hard for creators of any kind, who often are enamored with their metaphors, examples, exercises, and turns of phrase. But it's not about the content or curriculum or *mots juste*, but rather what will help the student. In the context of learning, there's no such thing as content that is nice to have. Everything is either critical to the understanding and success of your students, or an opportunity for them to become distracted, confused, or overwhelmed. A big part of what makes the Tony Marsh Method for language learning so effective, for example, is that it dispenses with much of what is generally thought of as core to the language (i.e. grammar), and instead focuses on the goal of functional fluency. So get clear on exactly what needs to be taught to achieve the learning outcomes and nothing more, and heed author William Faulkner's advice to "kill all your darlings" that aren't serving the students' goals.[204]

Now that we know what to teach, are we ready to move on to how? Almost, but not quite. First, there's an important second layer of the course design process to explore.

#2 SUCCESS BEHAVIORS: WHAT STUDENTS NEED TO SUCCEED

At the start of every year, aspirations for a happier, healthier life prompt countless resolutions to start going to the gym. This leads to a rush of gym memberships, but sadly, the majority go unused.[205] The same is true of the success rates of people who set out to quit smoking, learn to play guitar, and complete courses they've signed up for. The reason is simple: It's hard to change behavior. As the adage goes, "To know and not to do is really not to know." This poses a double challenge for educators in the era of volitional learning: We not only need to design learning experiences that empower students to apply and succeed with whatever we're teaching them, but also we have to design a learning experience that instills the behavior of *actually consuming and completing the course.*

> **A course that students don't complete, or one that students do complete but don't implement, is of little value.**

A course that students don't complete, or one that students do complete but don't implement, is of little value. For that reason, the second layer of Leveraged Learning is the success behaviors that will see the student through to the finish line. This is so important that out of a list of twelve research-informed strategies that "every teacher should be doing with every student," nearly half address specific success behaviors:

1. Give students more opportunities to reflect on their learning and performance.

2. Teach that the way students choose to study can hurt their ability to learn for the long term, and self-testing is more effective than reading notes. In other words, help students develop an awareness and understanding of effective learning strategies, so that they can take ownership of their own learning process.

3. Teach that sleep is critical to memory consolidation.

4. Teach students that effort matters most, and that neuroplasticity means they have the ability to rewire their brain to make themselves better learners.

5. Teach students to recognize how stress, fear, and fatigue affect higher-order thinking and memory via the limbic system.[206]

While the list of possible success behaviors is almost infinite, we choose the most important ones by thinking through what is most likely to prevent students from consuming what we teach and applying what they learn. Sometimes success behaviors are simple and logistical; for example, instructing students to block time off in their schedules each week to complete the course work is both easy and effective. But in other cases, this can be much more involved.

BUILDING FORTITUDE INTO EDUCATION

This is one of the areas where fortitude shows up most powerfully in education. If we know that students will encounter challenges, setbacks, and discouragement, we can arm them ahead to cope. This can be as simple as helping students anticipate what might happen and how they might feel about it, so that they have an effective response prepared. Peter Gollwitzer's research has shown that this "behavioral preloading" can be surprisingly effective, as recounted by Chip and Dan Heath:

> The psychologist Peter Gollwitzer has studied the way this pre-loading affects our behavior. His research shows that when people make advance mental commitments—if X happens, then I will do Y—they are substantially more likely to act in support of their goals than people who lack those mental plans. Someone who has committed to drink less alcohol, for instance, might resolve, "Whenever a waiter asks if I want a second drink, I'll ask for sparkling water." And that person is far more likely to turn down the drink than someone else who shares the same goal but has no preloaded plan. Gollwitzer calls these plans 'implementation intentions,' and often the trigger for the plan is as simple as a time and place: When I leave work today, I'm going to drive straight to the gym. The success rate is striking. Setting implementation intentions more than doubled the number of students who turned in a certain assignment on time; doubled the number of women who performed breast self-exams in a certain month; and cut by half the recovery time required by patients who had received hip or knee replacement (among many other examples). There is power in preloading a response.[207]

Consider the challenges that your students will face, devise a success behavior that can carry them through (ideally by looking at existing bright spots), and then backtrack through your curriculum to insert and instill those behaviors before students need them. With that in mind, we're ready to turn our attention to delivery.

#3 DELIVERY: HOW LEARNING WILL BE PRESENTED AND SHARED

When it comes to the delivery of a high-quality educational experience, there are many ways to get the job done. Say you want to teach how the modern economy works. Is your best bet to teach an extended college course on micro- and macro-economics, or write a series or research papers? Or would your students be better served by a 138-page narrative,[208] a 31-minute YouTube video,[209] or even combining online games with creative explanations?[210] The answer will depend on the specific objectives and students, but odds are that the brute force of long courses and research papers isn't the best way to go. To paraphrase a common saying, our students would benefit from our taking the time to create a shorter learning experience.

We must take the time to explore the metaphors and examples that best scaffold the learning that we seek to create, and we must consider the level of skill and fluency that our students need to achieve. Juliani and Spencer identify seven stages to the consumption and integration of knowledge:

1. The first, exposure and passive consumption, which leads to,

2. Active consumption, followed by,

3. Critical consumption, i.e. consumption combined with critical evaluation of what makes sense and how this fits into what the student already knows. This is followed by,

4. Curating, which is an active selection of which pieces are worth keeping and which pieces are worth abandoning. Then comes,

5. Copying and modifying, and then,

6. Mash-ups, which (like copying and modifying) involves taking something learned and making it your own. Finally, we arrive at the pinnacle of learning, which is the ability to,

7. Create from scratch.[211]

The upshot is that deep learning, real understanding, and the development of competence all involve the active participation of the student in the learning process. That doesn't just happen, it must be intentionally designed into the delivery of the curriculum. As articulated by Vai and Sosulski:

> Learning is not a spectator sport. Students do not learn much just by sitting in classes listening to teachers, memorizing prepackaged assignments, and spitting out answers. They must talk about what they are learning, write about it, relate it to past experiences, and apply it to their daily lives. They must make what they learn part of themselves.[212]

Find your metaphors, craft your explanations, and then create opportunities for students to practice and apply what you teach them, whether that's through activities or assessment. On the activities side of things, Vai and Sosulski offer a list of options, including discussions, journal writing and blogging, project-based learning, simulations, debates, portfolio building, offering critiques, conducting primary or secondary research, and delivering presentations.[213]

"They must talk about what they are learning, write about it, relate it to past experiences, and apply it to their daily lives."

If students can't immediately practice what you preach, a great tool in the teacher's toolbox is formative assessment with in-process evaluation of comprehension, learning needs, and progress. Offering this sort of frequent, low-stakes feedback on understanding helps students to consolidate and retain what they're learning. This is supported by the research of John Hattie, author of *Visible Learning*, who analyzed hundreds of meta-analyses of student achievement studies and found that formative assessment ranks third highest out of eight hundred fifteen factors.[214]

So far we've covered what to teach, how to support students through the process, and how to deliver the training. Now it's time to pack it all together into an effective user experience.

#4 USER EXPERIENCE: HOW STUDENTS WILL NAVIGATE THE LEARNING

For most of the past few centuries, the experience of education remained pretty much the same: A teacher at the front of a class lectured to room full of students. Sure, there was variation in terms of the expertise and visual aids of the teacher, the age and skill of the students, and perhaps the reference materials and note-taking equipment at their disposal. But by and large, the students showed up, listened to the teacher, wrote down their notes, and did some reading and homework, either alone or together with their peers.

However, in the past couple of decades, things have changed at a dizzying pace. The students may be remaining in a classroom, or sitting at home in front of their computer, or even out jogging and listening through their earbuds. The instructor may be delivering the lesson in real-time, or using a recording made weeks or years in advance. Students may meet in person to collaborate, or they may use a telephone, a messaging tool like Slack, or a videoconferencing tool such as Skype or Zoom. They may read books and articles, or watch videos, or listen to audio recordings, or even participate in virtual or augmented reality simulations. Students may be digital natives who are fluent in all these technologies, or baby boomers who feel bewildered by it all, or anywhere in between. The same is true of the instructor.

Navigating this landscape is challenging for two big reasons. The first comes down to technology; the landscape continues to change rapidly, and instructors feel as if they're constantly playing catch-up. Often they need to work with a myriad of tools of different levels of maturity, which may or may not coordinate smoothly. But this is a problem that will disappear with time. As learning expert Jonathan Levi shared with me when I interviewed him as part of the research for this book, "online learning in 2018 is where the Internet was in 2001. It's just a matter of time before we have things like pupil movement and dilation tracking to measure engagement, ECG readings to measure learning, and so on." Whether the technology gets quite that far, we can be confident that as technology matures, it trends toward an easier user experience. So we do our best, and over time our best gets better.

The bigger challenge is that of *frame of reference*, which puts blinders on our thinking that we don't even know are there. A case in point: Many North American educators implicitly assume that a single teacher can handle as many as twenty-five students. Where did this number come from? The surprising answer is a determination made in the twelfth century by the Jewish scholar Maimonides (who, incidentally, taught students in an oral tradition of chanting Torah and engaging in Talmudic studies. Not a typical classroom even in the twelfth century!). There are two categories of blinders that course creators must be extra wary of.

REAL-TIME AND IN PERSON VS. SEMI-SYNCHRONOUS AND ONLINE

The risk of taking education online and semi-synchronous is that we still design it as though it is real-time and in person. This means we create a poor man's version of an in-person classroom, which isn't a great learning experience. Here are a few features that are made possible by the semi-synchronous and online nature of modern education:

- Different students at different levels of skill and experience can concurrently work their way through adaptive learning paths, in a "choose your own adventure" flow-chart lesson hierarchy.

- Lessons don't have to be forty-five or sixty or ninety minutes long, nor do they have to be delivered on a weekly basis. Any lesson length is possible, based on what is best with the material, and any pace is possible, based on what is best for the students and the work they need to complete.

- Every student doesn't have to consume the training in the same way. Some can watch videos, some can listen to audio, some can read transcripts, and some can mix and match.

DESKTOP AND INTENTIONAL VS. MOBILE AND INTERSTITIAL

This isn't just a difference in screen; it's a difference in consumption pattern. This is a newer blinder, but no less challenging. For most instructors, when we think digital, we think computer, an assumption that is sorely out of date. Already the majority of Internet traffic comes from mobile devices, not computers.[215] This isn't just a difference in screen; it's a difference in consumption pattern. With computers we're typically seated at our desks, focused on whatever we're trying to do (like writing a book). With mobile devices, we're typically on the go, with our attention split between the content on our screen and whatever we've taken a short break from to attend to it.

Author Dan Pink describes how this has divided content into two broad categories: intentional and interstitial.[216] In the context of television, intentional content is the stuff that you wait to watch at home, on the couch, with your spouse beside you and a bowl of popcorn on your lap. Interstitial content, on the other hand, is the stuff that you'll watch in five-, ten-, and fifteen-minute bursts, while you're waiting in line at the grocery store, killing time in an airport terminal, or chilling out at Starbucks.

The implications for learning are profound, because inside most learning experiences are some components that require and justify intentional consumption, for example, the final assignment at the end of a module. Also, there's content that can just as easily be consumed in bits and pieces, like the lecture that can be listened to in four separate sittings. As instructors, we must be mindful of all this and intentionally design for it.

#5 ACCOUNTABILITY:
THE COMMUNITY AND TRIGGERS TO STAY ON TASK

On September 5, 2010, I joined twenty-one thousand participants at the starting line of the Montreal Marathon. It was a beautiful day, and we were all excited when the starting bell rang. I ran at a brisk pace, enjoyed the fresh air, and high-fived the volunteers at the early mile markers.

Then I started to get tired. The distance between racers increased as initially small differences in pace added to large differences in distance and time. I discovered that I hadn't trained nearly as long or hard as I should have, and I was feeling that deficit. But I pushed through, sometimes running, sometimes walking, but always moving forward. Around the twentieth mile, I hit "the wall," the sudden wave of fatigue that sets in toward the end of the race and threaten to crush you. I barely persevered and limped over the finish line with the thoroughly unimpressive time of about six hours. At many points along the way, I was tempted to quit. The race was long, I was tired, and my legs ached, so quitting would have been easy. Why did I keep on going?

Part of the reason was a commitment to myself, part was the context of all the racers all around me, and part was the accountability to all my friends who knew I was doing it. I would have to tell them that I had quit, and that was a distinctly unappealing idea. But the most important factor by a wide margin was that I ran the race with my then-girlfriend and now wife! This reversed the effect of an insidious challenge to behavior change: hyperbolic discounting.

THE CHALLENGE OF HYPERBOLIC DISCOUNTING

Daniel Kahneman was born in Tel Aviv in 1934, where his mother was visiting relatives. He grew up in Paris, France, and spent much of World War II on the run from the Nazis. After the war, in 1948, his family moved to British Mandatory Palestine, right before the creation of the state of Israel. He studied psychology at the Hebrew University in

Jerusalem, and then earned his masters and doctorate at the University of California, Berkeley.

The year 1977 was an important one for Kahneman. That year both he and his colleague Amos Tversky were fellows at the Center for Advanced Study in the Behavioral Sciences at Stanford University, and a young economist named Richard Thaler was there as a visiting professor. That sparked his interest in the burgeoning field of behavioral psychology, which led to ground-breaking work that won him the Nobel Prize in Economics, and was documented in his excellent book *Thinking, Fast and Slow*. The crux of his research was the strange apparent irrationality of human behavior, as a function of various cognitive biases. *Hyperbolic discounting* is one such cognitive bias, which is at the root of why accountability is so important in course design.

Hyperbolic discounting essentially means that we give more weight to consequences that are immediate than to consequences that wait for us further in the future. For example, given the choice between ten dollars today and eleven dollars tomorrow, most people choose eleven dollars. Given the choice between ten dollars today and eleven dollars next year, though, most people go for the ten dollars today. It's the logic of "better a bird in the hand than ten on the bush."

Hyperbolic discounting is the root of the challenge with doing coursework, training for and running a marathon, and pretty much every other thing that we want to do and know is good for us: the benefits are far off into the future, but the cost is right here, right now. Next year I'll be glad that I finished the marathon, but right now I feel like quitting. Tomorrow I'll be glad that I went to bed early, but right now I want to watch a few more episodes of *Game of Thrones*. As a species, we aren't very good at choosing what we *want* over what we *feel like in the moment*.

Accountability is so important because it reverses the effects of hyperbolic discounting, by adding both pleasure and pain that enforce the immediate decisions we actually want to make. Sure, my I'm tired and I feel like quitting this race, but I'm enjoying the company of my peers, and the physical pain of in my legs doesn't hold a candle to the emotional pain of quitting in front of my girlfriend!

Accountability, along with the community that provides it, is among the most important factors that keep us on target moving toward our goals. Conversely, a lack of accountability and structure is one of the greatest challenges in the transition from mandatory to volitional education; if I can choose to watch lesson materials and do the work on any day of the week, in any week of the year, in any year of the next decade, then the odds that I won't do it at all increase dramatically. This makes it incumbent on educators to build accountability into our learning experiences. A couple of easy ways to do this are forcing a minimum progression speed and raising the stakes:

Forced minimum progression. Sometimes the simplest solution is to take away some of that extra choice. Adding some structure to a program in which everybody starts on a certain date, must meet certain deadlines, and completes the program together can have a dramatic impact on completion rates, as is the case with Seth Godin's altMBA workshop[217] and my own company Mirasee's free Business Ignition Bootcamp.

Raising the stakes. This is implicit in the previous suggestion (such if missing a deadline has consequences), but can be taken to a whole new level. An extreme example is a commitment contract, described by Ian Ayres in his book *Carrots and Sticks*: committing yourself to donate money to a cause that you despise (an "anti-charity") if you don't meet your commitments. This draconian approach is effective but difficult to get students to get onboard. Thankfully, it often doesn't take that effort much to prompt action. For example, in one of the programs that my company offers, a missed deadline would add an icon of a frowning face to the student's course portal. There was no tangible consequence, but that frowning face was enough to affect student behavior.

Accountability is a powerful way to keep students moving forward, but be careful about applying it to compensate for other challenges in your course design. If students are getting stuck because of technology issues, the promise of an incentive or the threat of a penalty might be enough to get them to overcome the issue. However, it's often easier to fix the issue and eliminate the problem altogether.

#6 SUPPORT:
THE HELP AND COACHING THAT STUDENTS NEED

In 1984, educational psychologist Benjamin Bloom set out to measure the impact of mastery-based learning (meaning that students wouldn't progress to new material until they mastered the old material) and one-on-one tutoring on student achievement. He compared a regular classroom as the control with a lecture-based classroom that followed a mastery learning approach as variation A and a classroom with a mastery learning approach and one-on-one tutoring for students as variation B. The results were staggering: Variation A performed one standard deviation above the control, and variation B performed two standard deviations above the control.

"The average tutored student was above 98 percent of the students in the control class."

In Bloom's words, "the average tutored student was above 98 percent of the students in the control class." This was a true breakthrough: a way of supporting 98 percent of the students to perform substantially above the current average. The challenge, of course, is the lack of money and teachers to provide one-on-one tutoring to every student. Statisticians use the Greek letter sigma to represent standard deviations, which led to the naming of Bloom's 2 Sigma Problem: "to find a method of group instruction as effective as one-to-one tutoring."[218]

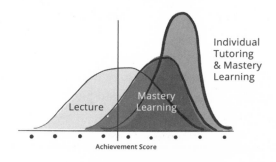

Lecture

Mastery Learning

Individual Tutoring & Mastery Learning

Achievement Score

Now, finally, technology and ingenuity are converging at a place where this problem can be solved. As Ryan Craig writes:

> Combining adaptive learning with competency-based learning is the killer app of online education. Students will progress at their own paces. When they excel on formative assessments integrated into the curricula, they are served up more challenging learning objects. And when students struggle, adaptive systems throttle back until they're ready for more. Adaptivity helps students build and maintain confidence, which leads to flow.[219]

The solution isn't just technology, but rather an intelligent integration and handoff between technology and human support. First comes mastery-based instruction, which means the student doesn't progress to lesson two until she's understood lesson one. The first step is to check on the comprehension and performance of a student and offer corrective feedback. This can be done not only by technology, but also be done by peers. As Coursera co-founder Daphne Koller explains in her excellent TED Talk, correctly structured and administered peer feedback structures yield the same returns to students as feedback from the teacher.[220] The best part is that students tend to learn the most from the process of providing feedback to their peers. When the peer feedback isn't enough, or a persistent issue arises, the feedback can be escalated to the support of a tutor or coach. The key isn't to avoid human support, but rather to apply it where it has the potential for the greatest leverage and impact.

So you start with content, layer on success behaviors, plan your delivery, design a user experience, craft elements of accountability, and offer support where it's needed. This is the recipe for a great learning experience for students, but still, an educator's job is never done.

DID YOU GET ALL THAT?
(LEARNING SELF-ASSESSMENT)

Want to test your understanding of the ideas that we just covered? Or start conversations with interested friends and colleagues? Here are a few questions to guide you:

1. What are the six layers of Leveraged Learning?

2. What are the four steps to determining the content of a course?

3. Researchers have found that "behavioral pre-loading" through implementation intentions is a powerful way to get people to follow through on their goals. How can this be applied when designing a curriculum?

4. According to John Spencer and A.J. Juliani, what are the seven stages to the consumption and integration of knowledge?

5. What is "formative assessment"?

6. Technology is advancing at a dizzying pace and creating blinders on educators' thinking about how to design learning experiences. What are are the two big categories of blinders that course creators must be extra careful of?

7. What are the two broad categories of content consumption according to Dan Pink? How are they different from each other?

8. What are two ways for educators to build accountability into learning experiences?

9. According to the research of Benjamin Bloom, which intervention resulted in student performance that was two standard deviations above the control (lecture-based classroom)?

10. What, according to Ryan Craig, is the "killer app of online education"?

11. What does an intelligent integration of technology and human support look like?

LIKE WHAT YOU READ, AND WANT TO GO DEEPER?

Here are a few good books to take a look at if you'd like to go deeper on some of the ideas presented in this chapter.

- Julie Dirksen's *Design For How People Learn*

- Peter Hollins' *Make Lasting Change*

- Marjorie Vai and Kristen Sosulski's *Essentials of Online Course Design*

For more information, including this entire book in digital format plus actionable conversation video guides at the end of each chapter, an expanded and up-to-date bibliography, and additional resources, visit LeveragedLearningBook.com

And if you'd like to work with my organization to apply the Six Layers of Leveraged Learning to your own courses as an instructor, you could consider the trainings and certifications listed at LeveragedLearning.com/sixlayers.

Where Do We All Go from Here?

A couple years ago, I had a few hours to kill on a layover in Chicago. I wandered the terminal, looking for something interesting. I mostly found fashion brand stores and restaurants, but then I found a store filled with a variety of tech gadgets, the unifying theme being "things that guys probably will think are cool." I entered the store and came across some *Star Wars* memorabilia, including an eighteen-inch-tall replica of Yoda, complete with white hair, green wrinkles, and tattered Jedi robes. It's ironic to say that a replica of a puppet appeared lifelike, but this one did.

When I approached for a closer look, its head turned slightly to face me, its eyes blinked, and it said in perfect Yoda syntax, "Teach you to use the Force, I will." I was impressed, and that was just the beginning. Yoda instructed me, "Extend your hand before me." So I did, hesitantly, not sure what would happen. The motion sensors at Yoda's feet combined with animatronic motors in his body combined to fling Yoda backward more than a foot, as though pushed by the Force emanating from my outstretched hand.

My first thought was, "This is so cool!" My second thought quickly followed, "I have to have it!" Fortunately my third thought countered, "Danny, this serves no purpose whatsoever. And it's a big box to lug through a terminal and continued business trip. And your wife will kill you." I just smiled and filed away the experience to share one day.

In all likelihood, my memory has embellished the story a bit, but the next part is clear: A few moments later I stepped into the men's room, and after using the facilities, I joined a row of guys standing in front of sinks, waving their hands wildly to find the exact angle and position for the motion-sensing faucet to sense their presence and turn on the water. The contrast was striking: The Yoda replica's sensors were so sophisticated that they made me feel like a Jedi for a moment, and a few paces away the faucet sensors were so lousy that it took ten minutes to wash my hands.

The future is here, it's just not evenly distributed.

This juxtaposition was a striking illustration of the story of progress. Digital Yoda was "amazing," and a few paces away stood a row of men muttering, "Are you freaking kidding me?!" The future is here, it's just not evenly distributed. The same is true of education and learning. That raises an important challenge for all of us: Even as we work to build a better tomorrow, how do we make the most of what is available to us today?

MAKING THE MOST OF EDUCATION, HERE AND NOW

I have a soft spot for Disney animated movies. As a parent, I appreciate their balance of entertaining children and holding the interest of adults; as an optimist, I appreciate their hopeful view that things work out in the end; and as an educator, I appreciate the life lessons that they embed in simple stories. For example, consider the Circle of Life lesson in *The Lion King*, shared in the unmistakable baritone of James Earl Jones as Mufasa: "Everything you see exists together in a delicate balance. As king, you need to understand that balance and respect all the creatures, from the crawling ant to the leaping antelope." Simba, the young lion who is heir to the throne, is puzzled. "But Dad, don't we eat the antelope?" Mufasa replies, "Yes, Simba, but let me explain.

When we die, our bodies become the grass, and the antelope eat the grass. And so, we are all connected in the great Circle of Life."

A similar Circle of Life exists in the world of education, with the three actors being learners, teachers, and businesses. Learners are instructed by teachers, who take cues from businesses as to what is needed and valuable in the work force. Those businesses then hire the learners.

Learner
(hired by)

Teacher
(teaching)

Business
(giving cues to)

What follows is advice to help each of these actors make the most of the opportunities available to us.

ADVICE FOR STUDENTS AND LEARNERS

As a young student or at the start of your career, your imperative is to make an investment in education that yields a worthwhile return in the form of acquired skills and increased employability. To that end, consider carefully whether the signal of a university degree—especially if it's not from a top school—is worth not only the cost, but also the opportunity cost. Remember that your time has value, and the opportunity cost of whatever else you could be doing if you weren't at school is estimated at $54,000. As a thought exercise, consider that if at the age of twenty-two, you invest $54,000[221] at a modest seven percent interest rate (which is the low end of the S&P 500 long-term average), by the time you're sixty-five, it will have grown to more than $800,000. Set that against the cost and debt that you might incur, and you'd better be confident that it's the right move for you.

Rather than a traditional college education, consider less expensive and more focused alternatives, for example, a hybrid program like the one offered by Minerva Schools at KGI; a "last mile" training offered by MissionU; find an apprenticeship, either structured through a program like Praxis (whose slogan is "The degree is dead. You need experience."), or independently, through a service like GetApprenticeship.com; or a coding boot camp such as Turing, Lambda, or General Assembly. They're all likely to serve you in much better stead than a generic college degree. Most of them cost substantially less, and some tie your investment directly to your future employability by charging little or nothing upfront, but being paid a percentage of the job wage you land when you graduate. The total amount is still much less than college.

> **Rather than a traditional college education, consider less expensive and more focused alternatives.**

If you're not sure what you want to do with your life yet, which is reasonable when you're in your late teens or early twenties, consider taking a gap year, either on your own or through a structured program like UnCollege. Take the time to expose yourself to new ideas and fields of interest, which can be done easily and inexpensively through online courses or with books ordered from Amazon or borrowed from your local library.

Another option is to do free work to gain experience or look for internships and apprenticeships. You don't need college to do this, and often the best positions must be found independently. To learn how to do this, look at Charlie Hoehn's *Recession-Proof Graduate.* His suggestions work just as well in good economic times and for people who never went to college. The decision to skip college or drop out can be walked back easily if you decide to do that later; most colleges offer generous, flexible sabbatical and leave options, in which you can take at least a year or two off with no strings or consequences. Harvard, for example, allows you to come back anytime. Although much is made of famous dropouts such as Bill Gates and Mark Zuckerberg, the truth is that they knew they could return. If it makes you more comfortable, rather than drawing a hard "I'm out" line in the sand, consider a "soft dropout" of a year or two to explore better options.

Also keep in mind that you can do a bit of college on the side. If the core value of the signal of a degree is that you have the keyword in your resume for automated application tracking systems to read, you can apply to college, be accepted, and maybe take a course or two, because most ATS systems can't tell the difference between "graduated with a Bachelor of Arts from Acme University" and "pursuing a Bachelor of Arts from Acme University."

Of course, the journey of lifelong learning doesn't end when you land your first good job. Make it a habit and a practice to keep learning, and stay engaged. Take courses that expand your skill set, and undergo training that challenges and broadens your thinking. There are countless examples of the former in every niche and industry. For the latter, some examples include Seth Godin's altMBA course, my company Mirasee's Business Ignition Bootcamp (which is free; details at LeveragedLearning.co/bib), and Byron Katie's training on The Work.

Make it a habit and a practice to keep learning, and stay engaged.

All of this will hold you in good stead and keep you both competitive and engaged. That said, the options available to students are only as good as can be created by dedicated and hard-working teachers.

Advice for Teachers and Experts

As a teacher and expert, your imperative is to stay current in your field, empower your students, and be well rewarded in the process. This begins by staying as active and involved in your field of expertise as possible. Read the news and the journals, follow the thought leaders, and do the occasional project or two. Without ongoing exposure, it's just a matter of time until you get left behind.

With your expertise secured, lean into your role as a teacher. Think deeply and be creative about what is most important for your students to learn, what scaffolding they need to wrap their heads around whatever you're seeking to share, and how to support them to encode that knowledge in a way that can be retrieved when they need it.

Most important, don't stop at knowledge. Layer insight and fortitude into your curriculum, and teach your students how to get where they need to go, with the *4 Cs* identified by the Partnership for 21st Century Skills: critical thinking, communication, collaboration, and creativity.[222] It can be a tightrope act to strike the balance between giving students everything they need, but not so much that they need not ask questions or reach their own conclusions. Follow the lead of the Turing School of Software & Design, as recounted by graduate Bekah Lundy: "They give you a lot, but they don't hand you anything on a silver platter."[223]

If some of these suggestions feel impractical because of the environment in which you work and teach, find or create an environment that gives you freedom to innovate, whether that means teaching elsewhere or putting out your own shingle as an educator entrepreneur. If you choose the latter, a good place to start is one of the Course Building Bootcamps offered by my company Mirasee (details at LeveragedLearning.co/cbb).

Finally, since we're still in the Wild West days of online courses and continuing education, do everything you can to lean into legitimacy. Work extra hard to ensure student success and capture those case studies. Align yourself with whatever bodies govern or lend credibility in your industry, and when you're ready, seek their stamp of approval. Most important, build connections with the stakeholders in your students' success. They include your students, but often they are businesses.

ADVICE FOR BUSINESS LEADERS

As a business leader, your imperative is to find good talent, retain those employees, and train them to produce the best individual performance and collective culture of innovation. The first step in that direction is taking a long, hard look at what really leads to success and performance, recognizing that university degrees aren't the key, and revising your job postings to reflect the stuff that actually matters. You won't be the first in doing so; in 2015 Ernst & Young professional

Grades in degree programs are "worthless as a criteria for hiring."

services in the United Kingdom removed degree classification from its hiring criteria, citing a lack of evidence that university success correlated with job performance.[224] Similarly, Laszlo Bock, former head of People Operations at Google, went on record saying that grades in degree programs are "worthless as a criteria for hiring,"[225] and currently as much as 14 percent of employees on some Google teams never attended college.[226]

Drop the application tracking system, or at least switch off the filtering related to education. While you're tweaking your hiring process, lean more into the assessments and simulations that actually give you a sense of what candidates can bring to the table. When Ernst & Young did this, they saw a ten percent increase in the diversity of new hires.[227]

Most important, cultivate the things that matter by developing a culture of learning and growth. Great books abound on this topic, ranging from Dan Coyle's *The Culture Code*, to Ron Friedman's *The Best Place to Work*, to Laszlo Bock's *Work Rules!*, and to Patrick Lencioni's *The Advantage*. Some of these authors can be brought to speak to your organization, and Patrick Lencioni's Table Group offers consulting and facilitation. Training also can be found from other providers, such as Mind Gym, The Center for Work Ethic Development, and my company Mirasee (focused on developing the strategic thinking skills of your employees and creating your own internal training; details at LeveragedLearning.co/business).

Most important, remember that talent comes in all shapes and sizes, and that the value of the degree you might have earned decades ago is very different from the value of degrees issued by institutions of higher learning today. As a business leader, it is your job to take the actions that lead your organization into the future, and this is how to do it.

THE REAL "GOLDEN TICKET" FOR EVERYONE

Among our time's greatest fonts of wisdom and inspiration is the red dot that sits center stage at the annual TED conference. Once reserved for the most exclusive and rarefied of attendees (those are still the people who attend the conferences), more than a thousand of these ten- to twenty-minute talks are available to watch online for free. So if you're looking for a jolt of energy and optimism, spend a few hours on a TED talk binge. The talks present a world of promise and possibility, in which changing your perspective can extend your life,[228] sense organs can be augmented or even replaced,[229] and great leaders inspire action by *Starting With Why*.[230]

Then we close our laptops, take out our earbuds, and return to our lives, in which millions of people face debilitating stress and anxiety, far too many struggle with disabilities, and business news is about more scandal than success. Looking at the world around us, we can't help but think wistfully of the hope offered in the TED videos, and wonder where it went.

The gap between the world that we live in and the world that we wish for is bridged by education. It's not by degrees, not by debt, and not by signals that aren't backed by substance. We need real education, which makes its beneficiaries more knowledgeable, more insightful, and possessed of the fortitude to see their way through challenges to reach innovation and success. That education is the real "golden ticket" for those who claim it, and with enough of these tickets in circulation, the ultimate winner is the whole of our global society.

As I wrote at the start of our journey together, every chapter in this book could have been an entire book, or several, of its own. Many of the ideas I've shared could be further expanded, and there's a lot of work to be done. That work is for all of us to do. Seizing this sort of education in its current early state takes ingenuity from learners, dedication from experts and teachers, and vision from business leaders. Most important, it takes courage from all three. I recognize that some of these changes are uncomfortable, and some are downright scary, just as it is for trapeze artists to let go of one bar in order to reach the next. But it's the best way for us as individuals to see the success that we want and need, and the only way for us collectively to build a better tomorrow.

"A responsibility we bear, and an opportunity we must seize."

When I taught my first college course in 2003—a seminar on "Race and Gender in Mass Media" at a top-ranked university—it looked very much like the courses I'd taken as an undergraduate a decade prior.

I'd stand at the front of the classroom each week and ask probing questions, hoping to engage my 20 charges. I'd lecture from, and periodically glance at, my printed-out notes. I certainly wouldn't screen a YouTube video (that hadn't been invented yet) or invite them to engage on social media (ditto). All assignments were handed in on paper, and graded by hand.

Fifteen years later, the landscape has changed almost beyond recognition, both for college students and for the adult learners I now work with.

I still teach traditional classroom-based executive education programs, primarily for Duke University's Fuqua School of Business. But I've also taught executive programs exclusively online, as well as in "blended learning" formats that mix webinars with an in-person component.

I've created online courses available outside academia, ranging from a 12-hour CreativeLive program on "Building Your Brand as a

Creative Professional" to a 35-minute online course, completed in partnership with *The Economist*, on "Reinventing Yourself Mid-Career."

I've developed more than a dozen courses for LinkedIn Learning (formerly Lynda.com), and have also created online courses that I sell directly to readers of my work, on everything from becoming a recognized expert to creating high-quality content more rapidly.

In short, I've experimented with almost every modern configuration of advanced learning, and have seen firsthand what works and what doesn't.

That's why I've found Danny Iny's work, and concept of *Leveraged Learning*, to be so valuable. For years, Danny has been a good friend and one of the smartest thinkers I know on the future of education.

I profiled him in my book *Entrepreneurial You* (Harvard Business Review Press, 2017), and followed his advice scrupulously when I was developing my own online courses, which have now generated multiple hundreds of thousands of dollars and impacted the lives of hundreds of talented professionals.

I've long agreed with Danny that our current system of education is broken. Back in 2013, I penned a *Harvard Business Review* article, "Grad School May Not Be the Best Way to Spend $100,000." Danny is spot-on that while historically prominent Ivy League schools will continue to prosper, and low-priced community colleges will continue to fill a targeted niche, there will be a massive shift in the middle coming very soon.

As he points out, "If an institution charges in the same range as Harvard and still sports unimpressive graduation rates, post-graduation employment rates, and low starting salaries for those graduates who do manage to find a job, the fact that they've easy to get into for people who want a college experience will no longer do the trick."

That means the "education-industrial complex" we've come to know for the past 70-odd years (since the end of WWII) is about to implode.

The challenge before us is how to navigate these uncharted waters—as professionals, lifelong learners, and (perhaps) as teachers, professors, and maybe even as course creators ourselves.

Danny's solution, which you've read in this book, is both wise and humane. For too long, many institutions (and individual instructors) took the easy path. They kept doing what had worked before, milking a profit and focusing more on their own needs or interests than what their students—their customers—wanted or needed.

Those times are past.

If we want to create a thoughtful, educated citizenry—and if we want, at a very basic level, for our own work to be effective and meaningful—then we have to get serious about understanding human behavior.

How can students, especially busy professionals who are now called upon to keep their own skills sharp over a lifetime, learn best? How can we create a learning environment that's engaging, empowering, and effective? And how can we, as learners, create the time and mental space necessary to continually refresh our knowledge and abilities?

Having read *Leveraged Learning*, I know you're better prepared to grapple with the critical questions we're all facing about the future of learning in the twenty-first century. As a professional, you understand the irreplaceable value of lifetime learning—the necessary ingredient to stay not just relevant but ahead-of-the-curve in the marketplace.

If you're also an expert and educator, you understand the critical importance of student engagement. It's insufficient—and in some circumstances, even exploitative—to create materials and then let students flounder them through on their own. We have to create robust learning communities, whether virtual or in person, that support student knowledge and growth.

And if you're a business leader, you understand that these issues simply can't wait. As the impact of technology and globalization deepens every day, we risk having a stagnant workforce ill-equipped to meet today's most pressing business needs. We can't rely on 'the system' to generate the high-skilled talent we need. We have to roll up our sleeves, get involved, and encourage and incentivize our employees to embrace transformative lifelong learning.

The shifts Danny has documented are disruptive, but carry within them the potential to reshape education dramatically for the better. It's a responsibility we all bear, and an opportunity we must seize.

Dorie Clark
Adjunct Professor, Duke University Fuqua School of Business,
and author of *Reinventing You*, *Stand Out*, and *Entrepreneurial You*
July 2018
New York, NY

Hey, it's Danny here...
I'm the book's author.

I hope you're finding it useful so far. Let me give you a few more ways to dig into these ideas:

Visit the book website. In addition to the entirety of this book, you'll also find additional resources, questions and videos to support discussion, an expanded and up-to-date bibliography, and more. Online at LeveragedLearningBook.com

Join a free Business Ignition Bootcamp. This training that my business periodically offers is designed to deepen your business insights and empower you to draw better inferences, and therefore make better decisions. Details at LeveragedLearning.co/bib

Join a free Course Builder's Bootcamp. If you're an expert with something to teach, we can get you started on the path to capturing that expertise, packaging it, and enrolling paying students. Details at LeveragedLearning.co/cbb

Check out our training programs for individuals and organizations at LeveragedLearning.co/training

P.S. Would you do me a small favor? A review on Amazon is always deeply appreciated. It will take you a couple of minutes and would mean a great deal to me.

ACKNOWLEDGEMENTS

We Came Together

As an avid reader, I've come across my fair share of acknowledgements at the end of books. It is customary for the author to make a show of how they couldn't have done it alone, and it really takes a village to shepherd a book to completion. I always read those paragraphs thinking "how nice of them to be so humble and gracious," because until you undertake a project as complex as writing this kind of book, you just can't fathom the extent to which the credit truly deserves to be shared.

The old proverb "to go far, go together" could not be more true; I'm incredibly proud of this book, and it is a reflection of all the people who were involved in making it happen. Except for any parts you particularly didn't like, that is; I'm afraid I have to claim all the credit for those.

High on the list of those deserving thanks are Abe Crystal, CEO of Ruzuku, and my team members Danielle Weil, Lexi Rodrigo, Austin Miller, and Rebekah Chalkley, who all helped with the drafting of key sections of the book. And especially my assistant Annie Brebner, who led the research team that painstakingly reviewed and annotated tens of thousands of pages of research material. And also the participants in our Leveraged Learning Intensive, who asked the questions and gave the suggestions that helped to refine my thinking around many of the topics covered in this book.

Thanks are also owed to the giants on whose shoulders I stood while writing this book—all those whose work I've learned from and referenced, and especially those who were so generous as to take some of their time to give me their opinions and perspectives on key issues: Dr. Sebastien Bailey, Ryan Craig, Josh Davies, Dr. B.J. Fogg, Jonathan Levi, Daniel Marcos, and Stever Robbins.

Special thanks go to Dave Lakhani for his mentorship and guidance, and Rohit Bhargava at IdeaPress for his diligent shepherding of this book from concept to final product. And also to Mitch Joel and Dorie Clark, who graciously lent me their names by writing the foreword and afterword.

And most of all, my family. Bhoomi, you are my partner at home, and my partner at work. You picked up so much slack while I was locked in the basement or a hotel room working on drafts, and I couldn't be more grateful. Priya and Micah, you've been more understanding than anyone could ask of a one or three year old that "Abba is working." Now that the book is finally done, I'm so excited to get back to picking you up from daycare every day, and I hope that the time away will lead to a better education and world for each of you, when you're ready to explore it.

About Danny Iny

Danny Iny is a lifelong entrepreneur, best-selling author, and CEO of the online business education company Mirasee. Best known for his value-driven approach to business, his nine published books include *Engagement from Scratch!*, *The Audience Revolution*, and two editions of *Teach and Grow Rich*.

Danny's lifelong love-hate relationship with education began with dropping out of high school at age 15, and eventually led to earning an MBA from Canada's elite Queen's School of Business. He has guest lectured at institutions including McGill and Yale universities, and is sought after by many authorities in the world of online business education, who are his private clients. Danny's work is followed by over 100,000 experts and professionals across various outreach channels (email, social media, blog, column on Inc.com, etc.), and over the course of 2015, 2016, and 2017 they've invested over $10 million towards training on the Leveraged Learning opportunity through his books and acclaimed courses, such as the Course Builder's Laboratory.

ENDNOTES

THE STORY OF PROGRESS (AND EDUCATION)

1. **Beginning of modern education in Europe.** The University of Bologna was founded in 1088, the University of Paris (later associated with the Sorbonne) was founded in 1150, and the University of Oxford was founded in 1167.

2. **Beginning of modern education in America.** Harvard University was founded in 1636, Yale University was founded in 1701, and Brown University was founded in 1764.

3. **Hot jobs that didn't exist?** This list was published in a posting on the employment site Glassdoor, and includes "futuristic" jobs like virtual assistant and Lyft driver. The full list is at https://www.glassdoor.com/blog/jobs-that-didnt-exist-15-years-ago/

4. **"Recent college grads are either unemployed or underemployed."** This is based on data shared in Todd Hixon's 2014 *Forbes* article "Higher Education Is Now Ground Zero for Disruption." Full article at https://www.forbes.com/sites/toddhixon/2014/01/06/higher-education-is-now-ground-zero-for-disruption/

5. **"Only a quarter of students find themselves working in their field."** This is based on data reported by Brad Plumer in the *Washington Post*. Full article at https://www.washingtonpost.com/news/wonk/wp/2013/05/20/only-27-percent-of-college-grads-have-a-job-related-to-their-major/

6. **$30,100 of debt!** The sad but true stat is taken from the Data Dashboard of Complete College America, a nonprofit that has been collecting nationwide data since 2010. Details at https://completecollege.org/data-dashboard/

7. **Tuition rising to $130,000 per year.** These projections were noted in a 2018 *Forbes* article "How to Save For Rising Education Costs and Potentially Get a Tax Deduction." Full article at https://www.forbes.com/sites/kristinmerrick/2018/03/06/how-to-save-for-rising-education-costs-and-potentially-get-a-tax-deduction/

8. **Taking Ivy League out of the equation.** Goldman Sachs makes a case against paying for an average higher education in this 2015 CNN article: https://money.cnn.com/2015/12/09/news/economy/college-not-worth-it-goldman/

9. **STEM Jobs.** The U.S. Department of Commerce stated in their *2017 Job Update* that STEM workers earn more on average. Read the report at http://www.esa.doc.gov/sites/default/files/stem-jobs-2017-update.pdf

10. **Higher education is $1.9 trillion out of the overall $4.4 trillion education market.** The higher education market is discussed on Inside Higher Ed, a website all about the American college system, at https://www.insidehighered.

com/blogs/technology-and-learning/19-trillion-global-higher-ed-market
and the overall size of the education market is reported in the *Washington Post,* at https://www.washingtonpost.com/news/answer-sheet/wp/2013/02/09/
global-education-market-reaches-4-4-trillion-and-is-growing/

11. **$1.4 trillion in student debt.** This frightening statistic, which places student debt as the second largest form of debt in the United States (second only to mortgages), is shared by Ryan Craig in his book *A New U.*

12. **6.8 million Americans are looking for work.** In a 2017 article on CNN, a discrepancy was shown between the 6.8 million Americans out of jobs, and the fact America had more job openings than ever before. Full article at http://money.cnn.com/2017/06/06/news/economy/us-job-openings-6-million/index.html

13. **15% completion rates for MOOC students.** Massive Open Online Courses have the potential to provide education at large scale, yet as shown in data collected by Katy Jordan in 2015, completion percentages are very low. Read more at http://www.katyjordan.com/MOOCproject.html

CHAPTER ONE:
WHY MODERN EDUCATION IS INEFFECTIVE, OVERPRICED, AND UBIQUITOUS

14. **5% of males born in 1900 held degrees.** This glance back at the history of higher ed is reported in chapter 4 of Paul Tough's best-seller *How Children Succeed.*

15. **40% of working American's have college degrees.** In an PBS Newshour article, reporters discuss how the greatest financial challenge for 18-49 year olds are facing is paying for that college degree. Read more at https://www.pbs.org/newshour/education/percentage-americans-college-degrees-rises-paying-degrees-tops-financial-challenges

16. **Academic inflation.** In a blog post by the University of Carlton, the concept of academic inflation explains why more and more people have degrees that aren't sufficient for getting a job. Read the full article at https://carleton.ca/edc/2008/thinking-about-academic-inflation-2/

17. **Lectures are ineffective.** An article by *ScienceMag* expresses that lectures aren't just boring, they are also ineffective. Students in lecture format classes are 1.5 times more likely to fail than those in active learning environments. Full article at http://www.sciencemag.org/news/2014/05/lectures-arent-just-boring-theyre-ineffective-too-study-finds

18. **What employers want.** A 2017 survey by Express Performance Professionals revealed traits that employers look for in their candidates. Having a degree is the least important factor on that list of considerations. Full data at https://www.expresspros.com/Newsroom/America-Employed/Survey-Results-What-Traits-do-Businesses-Look-for-in-New-Hires.aspx

19. **The majority of college grads have only "basic" levels of literacy.** This is addressed in chapter 1 of Kevin Carey's *The End of College.*

20. **"Failing to develop higher-order cognitive skills."** In their 2011 book *Academically Adrift*, Arum and Roksa discuss how college students are failing to develop the higher-order cognitive skills that they need to succeed.

21. **"Students fail to learn most of what they're taught."** Bryan Caplan's quote expressing that the materials universities are teaching have nothing to do with the labor market can be found in chapter 2 of his book *The Case Against Education*.

22. **In 2011, 50% of university grads under age 25 were unemployed or working in the service industry.** This sad state of affairs is discussed in chapter 2 of Ryan Craig's *College Disrupted*.

23. **In-house corporate learning centers.** The prime example is General Electric University, these in-house institutions take it upon themselves to educate their employees. This is discussed in the 2013 Boston Consulting Group report *Corporate Universities: An Engine for Human Capital*. Read more at http://image-src. bcg.com/Images/Corporate_Universities_Jul_2013_tcm9-95435.pdf

24. **Tuition growing at double the rate of inflation.** Ryan Craig continues to flesh out the discrepancy between the cost and use of a degree in chapter 2 of *College Disrupted*.

25. **"991 hours just to cover tuition!"** Also from *College Disrupted* by Ryan Craig.

26. **7 in 10 students graduate with an average of $30,100 in debt.** This is shown via 2017 statistics on the Complete College website. Learn more at https://complete-college.org/data-dashboard/

27. **Interest rates of 4.7% for undergraduate degrees,** and 6.84% for graduate degrees. This is shown via 2017 stats on the Complete College Website at https://www. accesslex.org/xblog/2017-2018-interest-rates-announced

28. **Opportunity cost estimated at another $54,000.** Also from *College Disrupted* by Ryan Craig.

29. **"Education is now priced as a luxury."** Klaus Schwab explains how a middle class job no longer guarantees a middle class lifestyle in *The Fourth Industrial Revolution*.

30. **Tuition rising to $130,000 per year.** These projections were noted in a 2018 *Forbes* article titled "How to Save For Rising Education Costs and Potentially Get a Tax Deduction." Full article at https://www.forbes.com/sites/kristinmerrick/2018/03/06/how-to-save-for-rising-education-costs-and-potentially-get-a-tax-deduction/

31. **No productivity gains, tuition to rise in perpetuity.** The 2014 *Forbes* article "Higher Education is Now Ground Zero for Disruption" quotes a previous President of Princeton University predicting that the cost of university will continue to rise. Full article at https://www.forbes.com/sites/toddhixon/2014/01/06/higher-education-is-now-ground-zero-for-disruption/#75e219ac1f89

32. **Only 20% of undergraduate student complete their degree in the set 4 years.** This shocking 2017 statistic pulled from Complete College website. More details at https://completecollege.org/data-dashboard/

33. **Overall graduation for 4-year institutions hover around 55%.** Graduation rate statistics brought to you by Ryan Craig in chapter 1 of his book *College Disrupted*.

34. **31 million Americans have some college credits but no degree.** This 2017 statistic was extracted from the Complete College website. More details at https://completecollege.org/data-dashboard/

35. **The majority of jobs come from small business.** This was reported by Steve King in a 2009 *U.S. News* article citing American Census Bureau information. Full article at https://money.usnews.com/money/blogs/outside-voices-small-business/2009/07/17/how-many-small-business-employees-are-out-there

36. **75% of recruiters use ATS technology.** This is reported by Capterra. Full data at https://www.capterra.com/recruiting-software/impact-of-recruiting-software-on-businesses

37. **"To question education is really dangerous."** Venture capitalist Peter Thiel comments in a interview for TechCrunch that it's hard break the illusion of the benefit of higher education in the U.S. Full interview at https://techcrunch.com/2011/04/10/peter-thiel-were-in-a-bubble-and-its-not-the-internet-its-higher-education/

38. **Higher education enrollment declined more than 6.5% in the last 5 years.** This statistic is shared in Adam Harris' 2018 article in *The Atlantic* titled "Here's How Education Dies." Full article at https://www.theatlantic.com/education/archive/2018/06/heres-how-higher-education-dies/561995/

39. **"Higher Education Is Now Ground Zero for Disruption."** In Todd Hixon's article for *Forbes,* he discusses the decline of higher education because there are too many things about the way they operate that don't make sense. Full article at https://www.forbes.com/sites/toddhixon/2014/01/06/higher-education-is-now-ground-zero-for-disruption/

40. **Closures, mergers, and shifts in focus.** In *The Atlantic* article "How Higher Education Dies," Adam Harris notes that the recent focus on the adult learning industry makes for a growing market. Full article at https://www.theatlantic.com/education/archive/2018/06/heres-how-higher-education-dies/561995/

41. **History of Worcestershire sauce.** Courtesy of the BBC, with more details at http://www.bbc.co.uk/ahistoryoftheworld/objects/mcraSW4BRJyBTtOMbcb6Tw

42. **How to use Worcestershire sauce.** For recipe ideas, visit https://www.thekitchn.com/5-ways-to-use-worcestershire-sauce-tips-from-the-kitchn-219380

CHAPTER TWO:
EDUCATION FOR THE AGE OF ACCELERATION

43. **Shift Happens.** The latest version of this video produced by Karl Fisch and Scott McLeod in 2008 about the rapid change brought about by digital technology and globalization can be watched at https://www.youtube.com/watch?v=u06BXgWbGvA

44. **Education must deliver an outcome that is meaningful.** This recounted by Kevin Carey in an interview with Paul Fain on Inside Higher Ed, about his book *The End of College.* Full interview at https://www.insidehighered.com/news/2015/03/23/kevin-carey-talks-about-his-new-book-end-college

45. **"Higher education has yet to adapt."** Joseph Aoun discusses this in his book *Robot-Proof*, describing the large gap between the existing education model and the changing economy.

46. **Self-driving cars.** The mileage self-driving companies have driven is tracked at https://medium.com/self-driving-cars/miles-driven-677bda21b0f7

47. **Trends in self-driving.** Automakers who are investing in the self-driving format are noted in this *Digital Trends* article, available at https://www.digitaltrends.com/cars/history-of-self-driving-cars-milestones/

48. **90% of traffic accidents are attributed to human error.** This statistic was extracted from a 2015 article in the Stanford's Center for Internet and Society. Full article at http://cyberlaw.stanford.edu/blog/2013/12/human-error-cause-vehicle-crashes

49. **3.4 million American person-years in commute.** Christopher Ingraham shares this statistic in his *Washington Post* article, calculating that the average amount of time wasted on a commute is 26 mins. Self-driving cars could redeploy this missed time more productively. Full article at https://www.washingtonpost.com/news/wonk/wp/2016/02/25/how-much-of-your-life-youre-wasting-on-your-commute/

50. **Millions of people work in the transportation industry.** In a report by the United States Bureau of Labor Statistics, employment by major sector is predicted for year 2026. Learn more at https://www.bls.gov/emp/tables/employment-by-major-industry-sector.htm

51. **Sensors for improving dairy herd management.** Thomas Friedman discusses the future streams of sensor technology in chapter 3 of his best-seller *Thank You For Being Late*.

52. **$55 million supercomputers in 1996.** Friedman notes the rapid development of computer technology in chapter 3 of *Thank You for Being Late*.

53. **$450 Radeon HD 3870 X2 graphics card.** Gizmodo reported on the development of this ATI product in 2008. Full article at https://gizmodo.com/349588/ati-breaks-teraflop-barrier-with-radeon-hd-3870-x2-gpu

54. *AlphaGo* **beat Lee Sedol in 2016.** In 2016 a computer program called *AlphaGo* beat the top ranked Go master at the game, as reported by Christof Koch for *Scientific American* online. Read more at https://www.scientificamerican.com/article/how-the-computer-beat-the-go-master/

55. *Libratus* **beat four top poker players in 2017.** In 2017, the *Libratus* AI developed by Carnegie Mellon University, beat the top 3 ranking poker players in the world in a 20 day marathon competition, as reported on the Carnegie Mellon news blog at https://www.cmu.edu/news/stories/archives/2017/january/AI-beats-poker-pros.html

56. **$1 million per mile.** This figure was shared by David Allen, AT&T's Director of Internet of Things (IoT), on an ad that ran as part of the *Masters of Scale* podcast.

57. **Robots disrupting the labor market.** Predictions about the disruption of the labor market are made by Martin Ford in the first chapter of his book *Rise of the Robots*.

58. **Jobs pulled in different directions.** Thomas Friedman describes the four directions in which technology will pull jobs in chapter 8 of *Thank You for Being Late*.

59. **Reports predict massive job loss.** In a 2013 research paper by Carl Benedikt Frey and Michael A. Osborne titled *The Future of Employment: How Susceptible Are Jobs to Computerization?*, they predict the automation of specific current jobs in the upcoming decades. Read the full paper at https://www.oxfordmartin. ox.ac.uk/downloads/academic/The_Future_of_Employment.pdf and in a 2015 quarterly report by McKinsey & Company titled *Four Fundamentals of Workplace Automation*, authors Michael Chui, James Manyika, and Mehdi Miremadi present statistics that demonstrate how 45% of current paying jobs could be automated by machines. Full report at https://www.mckinsey.com/business-functions/ digital-mckinsey/our-insights/four-fundamentals-of-workplace-automation

60. **Concern about jobs at risk.** In their 10,000 person survey, Price Waterhouse Coopers (PWC) reported on their website that 37% of workers are concerned that automation will put their jobs at risk. Read more at https://www.pwc.com/ gx/en/services/people-organisation/publications/workforce-of-the-future.html

61. ***Preparing for the Future of Artificial Intelligence.*** Joseph Aoun discusses this white house report in *Robot-Proof*, the original report being available online at https://obamawhitehouse.archives.gov/sites/default/files/whitehouse_files/ microsites/ostp/NSTC/preparing_for_the_future_of_ai.pdf

62. **The Budding Effect.** John Thornhill explains how the invention of the lawnmower in the 1800s by Edwin Budding sparked the later development of professional sports (that partake on fields), as part of a review of Frank, Roehrig, and Pring's book *What To Do When Machines Do Everything*. Read the review at https://www. ft.com/content/f4251416-2a76-11e7-bc4b-5528796fe35c

63. **Cynefin Framework**. In chapter 3 of *The End of Jobs*, Taylor Pearson discusses the four domains of decision-making context, as aligned with Dave Snowden's 1999 "sense-making device" research.

64. **The end of "bullshit jobs."** Historian Rutger Bregman's 2017 book, *Utopia for Realists*, is an argument for a liberal future that drives humanity forward.

65. **Children aren't being taught well.** Andrew Keen, one of the earliest authors to write about the dangers of the Internet, notes that 30% of people in senior positions have "no confidence" that schools are training capable future workers in his 2018 book *How to Fix the Future*.

66. **Teaching Psychological Freedom.** Venture capitalist Albert Wenger is homeschooling his kids, with the focus of teaching them skills that can't be replicated by a robot. As noted by Keen in *How to Fix the Future*.

67. **85% of job success comes from soft skills.** This statistic is reported in *The Soft Skills Disconnect* by the National Soft Skills Association 2015. Full article at http:// www.nationalsoftskills.org/the-soft-skills-disconnect/

68. **Hire for attitude.** In a 2012 article by *Forbes* titled "Hire for Attitude," Mark Murphy discusses the attitudinal deficits that lead to workers being fired

within 18 months of being hired. Full article at https://www.forbes.com/sites/danschawbel/2012/01/23/89-of-new-hires-fail-because-of-their-attitude

69. **Work attitude and self-management skills.** Peter Cappelli, speaking about what employers are really looking for, is quoted by Ryan Craig in chapter 7 of *College Disrupted*.

70. **Business Roundtable of employers ranking the most important work skills.** Ryan Craig explains in chapter 7 of *College Disrupted* how within a list of 20 skills an employer looks for in a new hire, skills taught in a traditional school setting are very low on the list.

71. **Critical thinking vs. degree.** As noted in Minerva University's book *Building the Intentional University*, 93% of employers are more interested in their potential hires' critical thinking skills than the presence of a university degree.

72. **Work ethic tops the list.** In a report posted by Express Employment in 2017, from a cohort of 1,030 employers, work ethic and attitude was rated as the most important trait for new hires. Full report at https://www.expresspros.com/Newsroom/America-Employed/Survey-Results-What-Traits-do-Businesses-Look-for-in-New-Hires.aspx

73. **More than 80% of respondents want leadership.** Joseph Aoun in *Robot-Proof* references the *Job Outlook 2016 report from the National Association of Colleges and Employers*, which is available at http://www.naceweb.org/s11182015/employers-look-for-in-new-hires.aspx

CHAPTER THREE:
THE CHANGING LANDSCAPE OF LEARNING

74. **Non-synchronous education.** The history and development of open and distance learning is discussed in a 2003 blog post for Athabasca University's International Review of Open and Distributed Learning. Full article at http://www.irrodl.org/index.php/irrodl/article/view/134/214

75. **Online dating.** Today nearly 1 in 5 couples that get married met online. This is from a 2017 review of online dating statistics on Zoosk. Full article at https://www.zoosk.com/date-mix/online-dating-advice/online-dating-statistics-dating-stats-2017/

76. **Online education advantages**. Bryan Caplan discusses the financial and engagement advantages of online learning in chapter 7 of *The Case Against Education*.

77. **"As far east as we could go."** Maureen and Tony Wheeler discuss the development of their company Lonely Planet in episode #6 of Guy Raz's "How I Built This" show on National Public Radio (NPR).

78. **Learning how to learn.** Former Harvard University president Lawrence Summers is quoted by James Bradshaw in a 2018 *Globe and Mail* article, saying that everything we are learning will become obsolete in a decade. Full article at https://www.theglobeandmail.com/news/national/time-to-lead/why-university-students-need-a-well-rounded-education/article4610406/

79. **"Figure it out on a daily basis."** According to Jeff Cobb, founder of research and consulting firm Tagoras, we now live in a "figure it out on a daily basis" economy, as noted in chapter 1 of his book *Leading the Learning Revolution*.

80. **"Just-in-case" education.** As Rohit Bhargava writes in his book *Always Eat Left Handed*, we either learn things at school because its traditional, or because one day we might need to know it.

81. **Learning can no longer be isolated to just undergraduate and graduate degrees.** This is argued by Joseph Aoun in his book *Robot-Proof*.

82. **The other 50 years.** Jeff Cobb explains that learning must be spread across our entire adult lives in chapter 1 of *Leading a Learning Revolution*.

83. **Open Loop Education.** The Stanford 2025 project explores what the future of education might look like, featuring a heavy focus on lifelong learning. Read more at http://www.stanford2025.com/open-loop-university/

84. **Students over 50 are the fastest growing contributor to the student loan market.** Stories of older age demographics going back to school for a mid-life career change are depicted in the 2018 *New York Times* article *The Snake Oil of the Second-Act Industry*. Full article at https://www.nytimes.com/2018/06/22/opinion/sunday/job-training-midlife-career-change.html

85. **40% of students are 25 or older.** In his book *Robot-Proof*, Joseph Aoun cites statistics from two pages from the Institute of Education Sciences (IES) and National Center for Educational Statistics (NCES): *Fast Facts: Back to School Statistics*, available at https://nces.ed.gov/fastfacts/display.asp?id=372 and *Table 303.40: Total fall enrollment in degree-granting postsecondary institutions, by attendance status, sex, and age* (selected years 1970 through 2025), available at https://nces.ed.gov/programs/digest/d15/tables/d15_303.40.asp?current=yes

86. **Light-speed learning.** In his book *Non-Obvious*, trend curator Rohit Bhargava discusses how much learning can be accomplished in "bite-sized" modules.

87. **"Last mile" education.** Ryan Craig coins the term in his book *A New U*, to describe the training needed to bridge the gap between foundational education and a career.

88. **"Anything you learn will be obsolete within a decade."** Former Harvard University president Lawrence Summers is quoted by James Bradshaw in a 2018 *Globe and Mail* article, saying that everything we are learning will become obsolete in a decade. Full article at https://www.theglobeandmail.com/news/national/time-to-lead/why-university-students-need-a-well-rounded-education/article4610406/

89. **Experiential education.** Dr. James Stellar discusses the concept and importance of experiential education in chapter 2 of his book *Education That Works*.

90. **No one is average.** To learn more about Todd Rose's research, read his excellent book *The End of Average*.

91. **Success of Udacity.** Sebastian Thrun left Stanford to start his own MOOC, Udacity, which currently has 1.6 billion users. Read more at https://www.smithsonianmag.com/innovation/how-artificial-intelligence-can-change-higher-education-136983766/

92. **Only 7% of students actually make it to the end of a MOOC.** This point is made by Max Chafkin in his *Fast Company* article, discussing the ins and outs of Udacity. Full article at https://www.fastcompany.com/3021473/udacity-sebastian-thrun-uphill-climb

93. **MOOC completion rates max out at 15%.** This data is shared in Katy Jordan's 2015 graph plotting the percentage completed versus enrolled in a MOOCs. More data at http://www.katyjordan.com/MOOCproject.html

94. **University of Phoenix course completion rates.** Even mediocre for-profit universities have a 17% completion rate for online courses, demonstrating that there are some major flaws with the MOOC model. This point is made by Max Chafkin in his *Fast Company* article, at https://www.fastcompany.com/3021473/udacity-sebastian-thrun-uphill-climb

95. **6 years over a lifetime.** This is presented in the Stanford 2025 project on the future of education, discussing open-loop education as a shift towards a longer, but far more incremental structure. Learn more at http://www.stanford2025.com/open-loop-university/

96. **Attention Span of a Goldfish?** In an article posted on Ceros in 2015, bloggers trace the internet trail leading to origin of the "humans have a shorter attention span than goldfish". Full article at https://www.ceros.com/originals/no-dont-attention-span-goldfish/

97. **altMBA's high completion rates.** Best practice in course design are drawn from Seth Godin's altMBA program by writer Stephanie Habif. Read more at https://medium.com/behavior-design/how-to-design-an-online-course-with-a-96-completion-rate-180678117a85

CHAPTER FOUR:
ECONOMICS OF THE NEW EDUCATION

98. **At least 80% of incumbents defeated their challengers.** This statistic was extracted from a 2011 government analysis of state and federal offices. Read more at http://economics.mit.edu/files/1205

99. **The turkey.** This story is drawn from Nassim Nicholas Taleb's 2008 book *The Black Swan.*

100. **Higher education is more than 40% of the overall $4.4 trillion education market.** The higher education market is discussed on Inside Higher Ed, a website all about the American college system, at https://www.insidehighered.com/blogs/technology-and-learning/19-trillion-global-higher-ed-market and the overall size of the education market is reported in the *Washington Post,* at https://www.washingtonpost.com/news/answer-sheet/wp/2013/02/09/global-education-market-reaches-4-4-trillion-and-is-growing/

101. **2.4 million fewer students enrolled than five years ago.** Ryan Craig reports decreasing enrolment numbers in American higher education institutions in the second chapter of his book *A New U.*

102. **"Success is correlated with a professor's ability to avoid teaching."** This quote is taken about incentives directing professors to research rather than teaching comes from chapter 1 of Ryan Craig's *A New U.*

103. **The accreditation industry.** Reporting on the state of the industry that accredits higher education institutions can be found at https://thebestschools.org/degrees/accreditation-colleges-universities/

104. **"A way for the merchant elite to distinguish their sons in society."** This reminder of the elitist history of higher education comes from chapter 10 of Ryan Craig's *A New U.*

105. **Only 21 cents of every tuition dollar are actually spent on instruction!** Ryan Craig reports this astounding fact in chapter 1 of his book *A New U.*

106. **The consolidation of major accounting firms to the "big four."** To be fair, they actually consolidated down to five, and then Arthur Andersen went out of business after the Enron scandal.

107. **Median American net worth of $44,900.** This statistic (very different from the average American net worth of $301,000) is reported by Tami Luhby in her 2014 article for CNN Money, which can be read at https://money.cnn.com/2014/06/11/news/economy/middle-class-wealth/index.html

108. **A third of all course credits are in only 30 courses.** Kevin Carey discusses the limited selection of course credits at higher education institutions in chapter 7 of *The End of College.*

109. **Endowments ranging from $22 billion to $38 billion.** Harvard has $38 billion, Yale has $26 billion, University of Texas System has $23 billion, and Princeton and Stanford each have $22 billion, as reported by the United States Department of Education at https://nces.ed.gov/fastfacts/display.asp?id=73

110. **More than the GDP of Morocco or Ukraine.** GDPs are per the International Monetary Fund (IMF), as reported on Wikipedia at https://en.wikipedia.org/wiki/List_of_countries_by_GDP_(nominal)

111. **Staffing is a $428 billion industry.** In a report by Statista, the global staffing industry revenue amounted to 428 billion U.S. dollars in 2016. Read more at https://www.statista.com/topics/4412/professional-staffing-in-the-us/

112. **Venture capital funds.** A prime example is Ryan Craig's University Ventures fund, dedicated to investing in startups working on opportunities in the education space.

CHAPTER FIVE:
LEARNING FROM THE EXPERTS

113. **189 channels.** In 2014 article posted on NewsWire, the Advertising & Audiences Report notes that average U.S. TV home only watches 17 channels despite having a record amount of options. Full statistics at http://www.nielsen.com/us/en/insights/news/2014/changing-channels-americans-view-just-17-channels-despite-record-number-to-choose-from.html

114. **The pace of book production.** According to the website Stuff Nobody Cares About (which is a misnomer, since I find this fascinating), there are on average 3

million books published each year. This is a stark contrast from the 9,260 books published in 1907. Full data at http://stuffnobodycaresabout.com/2012/01/31/how-many-books-were-published-100-years-ago-as-compared-to-today/

115. **130 million books in existence.** As Ben Parr wrote on Mashable, Google algorithms report there are 129,864,880 published in all of modern history. Full article at https://mashable.com/2010/08/05/number-of-books-in-the-world/

116. **15,000 books about Lincoln.** According to a 2015 Business Insider article, there are no less than 15,000 books that have been written about Abraham Lincoln in the past two centuries. Full article at http://www.businessinsider.com/best-books-on-abraham-lincoln-2015-2

117. **"Long Tail."** Chris Anderson described in his 2004 article in *Wired* magazine titled "The Long Tail" a simple concept with powerful implications. Full article at http://www.longtail.com/about.html

118. **Only 21 cents of every tuition dollar are actually spent on instruction!** Ryan Craig reports this astounding fact in chapter 1 of his book *A New U.*

119. **The effect of unbundling on revenue per student.** The consequences of the unbundling of courses from each other is discussed by Ryan Craig in chapter 6 of *College Disrupted.*

CHAPTER SIX: KNOWLEDGE: MAKING IT EASY FOR PEOPLE TO LEARN

120. **Spanish in a Month.** You can watch Connor Grooms' documentary for free at SpanishDocumentary.com

121. **Learning Spanish in a month?** Jared Kleinert's 2015 *Forbes* article highlights Connor Grooms, a blogger who has taken on learning different skills in a month such as DJ'ing and Spanish. Full article at https://www.forbes.com/sites/jaredkleinert/2015/11/30/this-20-year-old-teaches-us-how-to-learn-anything-in-a-month/

122. **Portuguese in a Week.** You can watch this documentary for free as well, at PortugueseDocumentary.com

123. **Declarative and Procedural Memory.** Learning mechanisms that enable us to carry out our day-to-day lives are discussed in chapter 11 of *Building the Intentional University.*

124. **Sherlock's Brain Attic.** Richard B. Hoppe writes in a *New York Times* letter to the editor that Sherlock Holmes would not have been surprised to hear that the brain has limited memory capacity. Full letter at https://www.nytimes.com/1999/08/03/science/l-sherlock-s-brain-attic-886041.html

125. **Gaps in our memory.** As Benedict Carey explains in chapter 2 of *How We Learn*, our brain prunes excess information so that it can retain the necessary amount of information in its limited space.

126. **Scaffolding success.** The success of scaffolding is demonstrated through the example of impressively productive learning interventions for children below average reading level, as documented in chapter 4 of J. T. Bruer's *Schools for Thought.*

127. **The Cone of Experience.** Edgar Dale's concept of a hierarchy of experiences and their effectiveness for learning, as recorded on Wikipedia. Full entry at https://en.wikipedia.org/wiki/Edgar_Dale

128. **Associative learning.** Benedict Carey exemplifies different situations in which people are able to better recall and remember material when there is an associative trigger present in chapter 3 of *How We Learn.*

129. **Far transfer.** Howard Gardner, the famous developmental psychologist, discusses the ability to apply information to a new context in his book *The Disciplined Mind.*

130. **Application in wide range of circumstances.** The importance of helping students apply learning across different circumstances is discussed in chapter 3 of *Building the Intentional University.*

131. **"Students rarely exhibit far transfer."** Aoun discusses the skill of far transfer in *Robot-Proof,* and highlights how many studies show that students rarely exhibit this skill, citing Ambrose, Bridges, DiPietro Lovett, Norman, and Mayer's book *How Learning Works.*

132. **Scaffolding in the Minerva curriculum.** Scaffolding is a large part of the structure of the curriculum of the Minerva Schools at KGI is outlined in chapter 3 of *Building the Intentional University.*

133. **Memory Palace.** The process of creating a visual mnemonic for learning complex facts and ideas. More details at https://artofmemory.com/wiki/How_to_Build_a_Memory_Palace

134. **Repetition and the "Forgetting Curve."** Benedict Carey discusses the power of repetition to encode memory in chapter 4 of *How We Learn.*

135. **Deliberate Practice.** This process of practicing the hard parts is based on the research of K. Anders Ericsson and documented in his book *Peak,* with co-author Robert Pool. The ideas are expanded upon in many books, including *The Talent Code* by Daniel Coyle, *Deep Work* by Cal Newport, and others.

136. **Illusion of fluency.** Carey explains how there is a discrepancy between really knowing the learning material or just recognizing it to the point of fluency in chapter 5 of *How We Learn.*

137. **Passive haptic learning.** The process of providing physical stimuli and feedback to facilitate and accelerate learning is demonstrated in this fascinating YouTube video: https://www.youtube.com/watch?v=dzYAOOYFVIO

138. **Spaced repetition.** A learning technique that incorporates increasing intervals of time between subsequent review of previously learned material in order to exploit the psychological spacing effect. Read more about this at https://en.wikipedia.org/wiki/Spaced_repetition

CHAPTER SEVEN: INSIGHT:
WHERE CRITICAL THINKING MEETS CREATIVITY

139. **Dillon Hill and Gamers Gift.** This story was recounted in the "how you built that" segment of episode #38 of Guy Raz's "How I Built This" show on National Public Radio (NPR).

140. **"Information is abundant; it's common."** This bold statement is made by George Couros in chapter 2 of his book *The Innovator's Mindset*.

141. **Cost of robotics.** Dmitry Slepov writes in his 2016 TechCrunch article about the high price of robots limiting their use in physical labor markets. Full article at https://techcrunch.com/2016/03/27/the-real-cost-of-robotics/

142. **Legal researchers being replaced by artificial intelligence.** John Markoff, writing for the *New York Times* in 2011, discusses how computer software and AI intelligence is making its way into tasks that were once exclusive to humans with decision-making skills. Full article at https://www.nytimes.com/2011/03/05/science/05legal.html

143. **Hollowing out.** Economist Paul Krugman, writing for the *New York Times* in 2011, explains that middle class medium-wage jobs have decreased while the two extremes have grown rapidly. Full article at https://www.nytimes.com/2011/03/07/opinion/07krugman.html

144. **Bad news for lawyers.** Richard Susskind explains in *The End of Lawyers?* that lawyers bill and work at high rates, but their work involves tasks of low expertise.

145. **Twice as many law school graduates as estimated job openings.** To be precise, that's 46,565 graduates vying for only 21,650 job openings. These statistics are shared by Joshua Wright in his 2014 *Forbes* article, at https://www.forbes.com/sites/emsi/2014/01/10/the-job-market-for-lawyers-side-work-on-the-rise-amid-continuing-glut-of-new-grads/

146. **Declining law school enrollment rates.** Writing for Above the Law, Staci Zaretsky writes about a rapid decline in applications to law school. Full article at https://abovethelaw.com/2013/08/law-school-applications-continue-to-tumble/

147. **"Canary in the higher education coal mine."** This quote about the legal profession comes from Ryan Craig, in chapter 2 of his book *College Disrupted*.

148. **Robot-proof education.** This segment is an encapsulation of the overall thesis of Joseph Aoun's *Robot-Proof*.

149. **The decision making antics of Alfred Sloan.** This story is recounted by Chip and Dan Heath in chapter 5 of *Decisive*.

150. **"When two men always agree, one of them is unnecessary."** William Wrigley Jr.'s famous quote was uncovered by Quote Investigator. Full article at https://quoteinvestigator.com/2015/04/04/agree/

151. **"Tell me something that's true that nobody agrees with."** Writing for *Forbes* in 2014, Robert Hof shares this advice from venture capitalist Peter Thiel to entrepreneurs. Full article at https://www.forbes.com/sites/roberthof/2014/02/27/peter-thiels-advice-to-entrepreneurs-tell-me-something-thats-true-but-nobody-agrees-with/

152. **"Our brains are challenged by novelty."** This quote comes from chapter 1 of Dr. Elkhonon Goldberg's *Creativity*.

153. **The "mere exposure" effect.** This social psychology phenomenon is described in a 2008 article on *Psychology Today*, available at https://www.psychologytoday.com/ca/blog/ulterior-motives/200811/know-me-is-me-i-mere-exposure

154. **The cost of breaking a record.** The surprising financial effort that it takes to get a record on the radio is described on music blog Making It Mag, at https://www.makinitmag.com/blog/music-101/how-much-does-it-really-cost-break-new-record-answer-might-shock-you

155. **Musicians working with Zumba.** Zumba co-founders Alberto "Beto" Perez and Alberto Perlman discuss musicians wanting to use Zumba to promote their music in episode #41 of Guy Raz's "How I Built This" show on National Public Radio (NPR).

156. **Critical thinking valued more than a university degree.** The statistic that 93% of employers value critical thinking skills over an undergraduate degree comes from chapter 3 of *Building the Intentional University*.

157. **Definition of Critical Thinking.** This comes from CriticalThinking.org. Full definition at http://www.criticalthinking.org/pages/our-conception-of-critical-thinking/411

158. **Academically adrift.** Aoun reports in *Robot-Proof* on research by Richard Arum and Josipa Roska that students are failing to acquire higher order thinking skills at university, documented in their 2011 book *Academically Adrift*.

159. **"Harvard is telling MBA students what to think."** Duff McDonald argues that the case study method, often practiced in business schools, fails to foster any higher order cognitive skills in chapter 5 of *The Golden Passport*.

160. **"Most business schools are adept at teaching respondent behavior."** Also from Duff McDonald's *The Golden Passport*.

161. **The Minerva curriculum.** The work being done at the Minerva Schools at KGI are documented in detail in the book *Building the Intentional University*.

162. **Steve Jobs' famous commencement speech to the Stanford graduating class of 2005** is immortalized on the TED website at https://www.ted.com/talks/steve_jobs_how_to_live_before_you_die

163. **Creativity comes in many shapes and sizes.** The multiple forms creativity can take are noted in chapter 1 of John Spencer and A.J. Juliani's book *Launch*.

164. **Ingredients of the creative process.** Elkhonon Goldberg discusses the varying constructs that collaborate with and foster creativity in his book *Creativity*.

165. **"It's uncomfortable to focus so intently on what you're bad at."** It is imperative to practice the parts of skills that you find most challenging, but also very difficult. Paul Tough explores this in chapter 3 of *How Children Succeed*.

166. **"Creativity is not mysterious."** Keith Sawyer explains in his book *Zig Zag* that creative people lean on routine in their day to day to foster creative behavior and output.

167. **The creative process.** Keith Sawyer breaks down the actions one can take to foster creativity, by identifying eight stages of the creative process in Zig Zag

168. **Importance of incubation.** Graham Wallas' 1926 research on the importance of incubation is documented by Benedict Carey in *How We Learn*.

CHAPTER EIGHT: FORTITUDE:
HOW THE TOUGH KEEP GOING WHEN THE GOING GETS TOUGH

169. **College drop-out rates.** Data reporting first-year drop-out rates in the United States were collected in 2014 by the National Student Clearinghouse Research Centre. Learn more at https://nscresearchcenter.org/snapshotreport-persistenceretention22/

170. **MOOC completion rates.** In a 2015 report, Katy Jordan shares data representing completions rates of Massive Open Online Courses that shows that roughly 15% of students complete these offerings. Full report at http://www.katyjordan.com/MOOCproject.html

171. **High online course drop-out rates.** Online courses have drop-out rates in the high 80th percentile. Details at https://novoed.com/blog/1050/a-strategy-for-increasing-completion-rates/

172. **Winners also quit.** In a 2008 *New York Times* article, Seth Godin, author of *The Dip*, points out that winners quit the right things. Full article at https://www.nytimes.com/2008/08/16/business/16shortcuts.html

173. **3 Ps of Pessimism.** Positive Psychologist Martin Seligman's 3 Ps of Pessimism are outlined by the Positive Psychology Program on their website at https://positivepsychologyprogram.com/explanatory-styles-optimism/

174. **Solving malnutrition in Vietnam.** The amazing story of finding community leaders that can demonstrate what works rather than trying to solve for what doesn't is recounted by Pascale, Sternin & Sternin in *The Power of Positive Deviance*.

175. **Finding the Bright Spots.** Dan Heath, co-author of *Switch*, describes in an interview on *Fast Company* how to find "bright spots" by identifying leaders in their environment and cloning their processes. Full article at https://www.fastcompany.com/1634997/dan-heath-how-find-bright-spots

176. **Deliberate Practice.** K. Anders Ericsson explains the concept of deliberate practice in his book *Peak*. Deliberate practice can be seen as pushing yourself, or stepping out of your comfort zone in a learning context.

177. **2.5% to 3% of the population is gifted.** This is a statistical extrapolation of the definition of gifted being two standard deviations above the norm, explained by Anya Kamenetz in her 2015 NPR article about identifying and fostering gifted students in K-12 learning experiences. Full article at https://www.npr.org/sections/ed/2015/09/28/443193523/who-are-the-gifted-and-talented-and-what-do-they-need

178. **4.5% of high-school dropouts are gifted.** This statistic comes from Esra Kaskaloglu's 20003 paper *Gifted Students Who Drop Out: Who and Why: A Meta-Analytical Review of the Literature*, presented in Proceedings of the Hawaii International Conference on Education.

179. **Online course retention rates.** These figures are discussed by Papia Bawa in a 2016 academic article in Sage Journals, which can be found at http://journals.sagepub.com/doi/full/10.1177/2158244015621777

180. **"Grades reflect life skills."** In this Literature Review featuring research from the University of Chicago, grades reflect a variation of students work habits and behaviors, but also how they feel about themselves: https://files.eric.ed.gov/fulltext/ED542543.pdf

181. **"More than smarts are required for success."** This from *Schools, Skills, and Synapses* by economist James J. Heckman, who explains that having fortitude plays a big factor in being successful. Details at http://jenni.uchicago.edu/papers/Heckman_2008_EI_v46_n3.pdf

182. **High adversity with high support.** That children who experience both adversity and support also develop fortitude is discussed by Sherry and Rob Walling in *The Entrepreneur's Guide to Keeping Your Sh*t Together.*

183. **Only 4 NBA players under 5'10" since 2010.** Earl Boykins is 5'5," and Nate Robinson, Isaiah Thomas, and Kay Felder are all 5'9." Wikipedia: https://en. wikipedia. org/wiki/List_of_ shortest_players_in_National_ Basketball_Association_history

184. **4 non-cognitive factors and 4 key mindsets.** Described in chapter 9 of Whitman and Kelleher's *Neuroteach.*

185. **Nobody is gritty about everything.** Caroline Adams Miller explains in *Getting Grit* that we can only be gritty about things that we care about.

186. **Intrinsically motivated people try harder and longer.** Angela Duckworth, leading grit psychologist, discusses how intrinsic interest fosters perseverance in chapter 5 of *Grit.*

187. **Intrinsic vs. extrinsic motivation.** This tradeoff and debate is discussed in a 2004 academic essay published by School Psychology Review. Full essay at https://www. misd.net/mtss/consequences/extrinsic_rewards.pdf

188. **Three elements of mindfulness.** Psychologists Shauna Shapiro, Linda Carlson, John Astin, and Benedict Freedman discuss their three mechanisms of mindfulness in a research article printed in the Journal of Clinical Psychology in 2006. Full article at http://citeseerx.ist.psu.edu/viewdoc/download?doi=10.1.1.470.370 9&rep=rep1&type=pdf

189. **WOOP Process.** Gabriele Oettingen develops a unique method to help achieve your goals in Rethinking Positive Thinking: Inside the New Science of Motivation https://www.amazon.com/ Rethinking-Positive-Thinking- Science-Motivation-ebook/dp/ B00INIXT4

CHAPTER NINE:
DESIGNING GREAT COURSES

190. **Einstein was a good student.** According to this photograph of Einstein's report card from 1879, he got good grades. Full article at https://gizmodo.com/5884050/einstein-actually-had-excellent-grades

191. **Einstein's supportive mother.** Einstein's mother's supportive parenting skills had a great effect on his learning, as documented at https://www.theodysseyonline.com/strive-albert-einsteins-mother

192. **Designing the perfect shopping cart.** In a 1999 episode of ABC Nightline, design firm IDEO reinvents the classic shopping cart. Full video at https://www.youtube.com/watch?v=M66ZU2PCICM

193. **Building a better cubicle.** In a 2002 feature on CBS, the design firm IDEO is challenged to build a better cubicle. Watch the video at https://www.youtube.com/watch?v=iuzMTw37psg

194. **LAUNCH.** The acronym explaining "design thinking" is from chapter 3 of *Empower* by Spencer and Juliani.

195. *Salvator Mundi sold for $450 million.* The sale of Da Vinci's painting of Jesus Christ for a record $450 million is documented at https://metro.co.uk/2017/11/16/leonardo-da-vinci-portrait-of-jesus-christ-salvator-mundi-sells-for-450000000-7083091/

196. **Michelangelo was a millionaire.** In a 2002 article by the Telegraph, a study by Italy's National Institute of Renaissance Studies discusses their findings that Michelangelo denied himself of all comfort despite being a multi-millionaire in the 1500s. Full article at https://www.telegraph.co.uk/news/worldnews/europe/italy/1414836/Michelangelo-is-branded-a-multi-millionaire-miser.html

197. **The "Beta Mentality."** This concept is described by Jeff Cobb in chapter 9 of *Leading the Learning Revolution*.

198. **Every teacher needs real feedback.** Bill Gates makes a strong case for investing in teacher feedback in his 2013 TED talk, which can be watched at https://www.ted.com/talks/bill_gates_teachers_need_real_feedback

199. **Rider, elephant, path.** This metaphor was developed by Jonathan Haidt in his book *The Happiness Hypothesis*, and was later popularized by Chip and Dan Heath in *Switch*.

200. **The Hierarchy of User Friction.** This framework is presented by Sachin Rekhi, CEO of Notejoy, in his article at https://medium.com/@sachinrekhi/the-hierarchy-of-user-friction-e99113b77d78

201. **Losing $1.6 billion per second.** In an article posted on *Fast Company* in 2012, Amazon predicted that they would lose $1.6 billion in sales should their site operate even one second slower. Full article at https://www.fastcompany.com/1825005/how-one-second-could-cost-amazon-16-billion-sales

202. **Reducing interaction friction.** Also from Sachin Rekhi's "Hierarchy of User Friction" article at https://medium.com/@sachinrekhi/the-hierarchy-of-user-friction-e99113b77d78

203. **Backward-Integrated Design.** This approach to course design is highlighted by Chip and Dan Heath in their 2017 book *The Power of Moments*.

CHAPTER TEN:
THE SIX LAYERS OF LEVERAGED LEARNING

204. Working backwards to design courses. This process is laid out by Vai and Sosulski in chapter 9 of *Essentials of Online Course Design*.

205. Gym memberships. A 2016 *USA Today* article reports that 67% of gym memberships are never put to use. Full article at https://www.usatoday.com/story/money/personalfinance/2016/04/27/your-gym-membership-good-investment/82758866/

206. Teaching strategies. Whitman and Kelleher propose in *Neuroteach* the top 12 research-based strategies that teachers should be implementing in their classrooms.

207. Behavioral pre-loading. Peter Gollwitzer's research is described by Chip and Dan Heath in *The Power of Moments*.

208. Narrative about economics. A great source for learning about the basics of economics is Ben Mathew's book *Economics: The Remarkable Story of How the Economy Works*.

209. YouTube video about economics. Ray Dalio presents a 30-minute video on the principles of economics. Full video at https://www.youtube.com/watch?v=PHeobxAIuko

210. Economics games. A 2012 *Forbes* article highlights education-based economics games that can teach children about world markets and exchange rates. Full article at https://www.forbes.com/sites/moneywisewomen/2012/05/01/how-online-gaming-can-teach-kids-about-the-economy/

211. Seven stages of consumption and knowledge integration. From Spencer and Juliani's book *Empower*.

212. Learning is not a spectator sport. Vai and Sosulski discuss how students need to take an active part in their learning in chapter 5 of *Essentials of Online Course Design*.

213. Activities for students to practice. From Vai and Sosulski, in chapter 6 of *Essentials of Online Course Design*.

214. Meta-analysis of student achievement. The analysis leading to the realization of the importance of formative assessment is documented in John Hattie's book *Visible Learning*.

215. Majority of internet traffic is mobile. Statista, the Statistics Portal, presents 2018 data that mobile internet traffic is more common than computer traffic. Details at https://www.statista.com/statistics/277125/share-of-website-traffic-coming-from-mobile-devices/

216. Intentional vs. interstitial content. In a 2018 article in *The Atlantic,* Daniel Pink describes two different types of content: intentional, and interstitial. Full article at https://www.theatlantic.com/technology/archive/2018/06/the-future-of-television-is-being-able-to-pick-shows-by-length/562547/

217. Forced minimum progression in altMBA. Stephanie Habif's article discusses how to design a course with high completion rates. Seth Godin's altMBA is a great example of these practices. Full article on https://medium.com/behavior-design/how-to-design-an-online-course-with-a-96-completion-rate-180678117a85

218. **Bloom's 2 Sigma Problem.** See Wikipedia: https://en.wikipedia.org/wiki/Bloom%27s_2_Sigma_Problem

219. **Technology and ingenuity are converging.** Ryan Craig discusses the combination of adaptive learning with competency-based learning in online course design in chapter 5 of *College Disrupted.*

220. **Peer grading and feedback.** In her 2012 TED Talk, Coursera co-founder Daphne Koller describes how effectively administered peer grading structures can work and scale. https://www.ted.com/ talks/daphne_koller_what_we_ re_learning_ from_online_ education

WHERE DO WE ALL GO FROM HERE?

221. **Opportunity cost of school.** Ryan Craig reports in chapter 2 of *College Disrupted* that the time invested in college equates to an opportunity cost of roughly $54,000.

222. **4 Cs: Critical Thinking, Communication, Collaboration, and Creativity.** These 21st century skills are highlighted in chapter 4 of Wojcicki and Izumi's *Moonshots in Education.*

223. **The Turing School of Software & Design.** In episode 31 of Nat Eliason's "Nat Chat" podcast, Turing alumnus Bekah Lundy describes her experience. Full episode at https://www.nateliason.com/bekah-lundy/

224. **Weak correlation between university success and job performance.** This data is shared by Ryan Craig in chapter 3 of *A New U.*

225. **"G.P.A.'s are worthless as a criteria for hiring."** As reported in a 2013 *New York Times* article, which can be read at https://www.nytimes.com/2013/06/20/business/in-head-hunting-big-data-may-not-be-such-a-big-deal.html

226. **14% of employees on some Google teams never attended college.** As reported by Ryan Craig in chapter 3 of *A New U.*

227. **Increased diversity at Ernst & Young.** The impact of alternative, skill-based hiring processes on diversity are highlighted by Ryan Craig in chapter 3 of *A New U.*

228. **Changing your perspective can extend your life.** Psychologist Kelly McGonigal discusses the surprising effects of a new perspective on stress in her 2013 TED Talk. Watch the video at https://www.ted.com/talks/kelly_mcgonigal_how_to_make_stress_your_friend

229. **Sense organs can be augmented or even replaced.** Neuroscientist David Eagleman dissects human senses; Daniel Kish, who went blind at 13 months of age, explains to his viewers how he uses echolocation to see; and Dr. Sheila Nirenberg discusses prosthetic sensory devices; watch the videos at https://www.ted.com/talks/david_eagleman_can_we_create_new_senses_for_humans, https://www.ted.com/talks/daniel_kish_how_i_use_sonar_to_navigate_the_world, and https://www.ted.com/talks/sheila_nirenberg_a_prosthetic_eye_to_treat_blindness

230. **Great leaders inspire action.** Simon Sinek, author of *Start With Why*, discusses how leadership can inspire cooperation in his 2009 TED Talk. Watch the video at https://www.ted.com/talks/simon_sinek_how_great_leaders_inspire_action

INDEX